SUCCESSFUL **SG** GARDENING

PLANT
PARTNERS

Staff for Successful Gardening (U.S.A.)
Senior Associate Editor: Carolyn T. Chubet
Editorial Assistant: Vita Gardner

Contributors
Editor: Thomas Christopher
Art Editor: Richard Boddy
Editorial Assistant: Troy Dreier
Consulting Editor: Lizzie Boyd (U.K.)
Consultants: Dora Galitzki, Matt Horn
Copy Editor: Sue Heinemann
Art Assistant: Antonio Mora

READER'S DIGEST GENERAL BOOKS
Editor in Chief: John A. Pope, Jr.
Managing Editor: Jane Polley
Executive Editor: Susan J. Wernert
Art Director: David Trooper
Group Editors: Will Bradbury, Sally French,
Norman B. Mack, Kaari Ward
Group Art Editors: Evelyn Bauer, Robert M. Grant, Joel Musler
Chief of Research: Laurel A. Gilbride
Copy Chief: Edward W. Atkinson
Picture Editor: Richard Pasqual
Head Librarian: Jo Manning

The credits and acknowledgments that appear on page 176
are hereby made a part of this copyright page.

Library of Congress Cataloging in Publication Data
Plant Partners.
       p.   cm. — (Successful gardening)
   Includes index.
   ISBN 0-89577-614-6 — ISBN 0-89577-961-7 (pbk)
   1. Companion planting.   I. Reader's Digest Association.
II. Series.
SB453.6.P58   1994
635.9—dc20   94-13509

Printed in the United States of America

Opposite: A long-lasting partnership consisting of tall *Euphorbia characias
wulfennii* above clumps of bright yellow *E. polychroma* and daisy-flowered
Argyranthemum 'Jamaica Primrose' achieves flower
harmony and pleasing foliage contrast.

Overleaf: Backed by climbers and wall shrubs, a summer medley of pinks
and blues including lilies, roses, lavenders, and phlox, grow in happy
companionship. They are tempered by white petunias and fronted by
bedding plants and ground-hugging alpines.

THE READER'S DIGEST ASSOCIATION, INC.
Pleasantville, New York / Montreal

SUCCESSFUL **SG** GARDENING

PLANT
PARTNERS

CONTENTS

Tree partners White willow, sycamore, and Japanese maple guard conifers, shrubs, and colorful perennials.

Tree options

Among the many reasons for choosing and planting trees in a garden is the fact that no other plants have as much visual impact. Trees define a garden's structure and content. They can add height to a flat landscape as well as help to obscure eyesores. They also introduce sound and movement to the garden and filter winds and external noises.

Numerous garden trees are available. When making a selection, first consider the size and shape of your lot. Always bear in mind the eventual height and spread of the mature tree. The beautiful mountain silverbell *(Halesia monticola),* for example, may be purchased as a slender sapling, but after 20 years it may reach a height of 40 ft (12 m), with an even wider spread. Fortunately, there are trees for every garden. They range from narrow columns to round-headed varieties, from low and spreading Japanese maples for small gardens to weeping willows that cast shade on warm summer days. In addition, you can choose between deciduous trees and evergreens, gay, flowering species, and solemn conifers. Leaves come in every shade of green, as well as golden, gray, purple, and variegated colors.

The beauty of trees is evident throughout the year — from the elegant tracery of gleaming white birch trunks in winter, to the delicate blossoming of cherries and crab apples in spring, the textured, colored barks of maples in summer, and the glorious colors and clustered berries of mountain ashes in fall. Golden yews, blue spruces, and sculptural hollies offer their calming presence all year round.

In large gardens, trees planted in groups have the greatest visual impact. In smaller gardens, one well-chosen specimen tree becomes an instant focal point, especially when it is partnered by low growing shrubs, ornamental grasses, and perennials or underplanted with spring-flowering bulbs and bedding annuals.

Living trees An old fruit tree supporting a clematis spreads dappled shade over spring bulbs and foliage perennials.

TREE TEAM-UP

Give your trees impact with striking partners and clever underplanting, or group them for an impressive show.

Deciduous trees grown for the beauty of their leaves, flowers, or fruit are often partnered with early flowers, particularly bulbs, that bloom before the trees are in full leaf. Alternatively, they can be underplanted with shade-tolerant, ground-covering perennials and shrubs, or placed among evergreen trees of contrasting shape and foliage.

As an example, the arching Mount Etna broom *(Genista aethnensis),* which bears scented yellow pea flowers in midsummer, makes a handsome contrast with the pillarlike chamaecyparis, and is airy enough for summer annuals to flower beneath it.

Trees with brilliant fall tints can create stunning pictures. For rich color contrast, plant a paper birch *(Betula papyrifera),* with its yellow leaves and peeling white bark, next to a Japanese maple *(Acer palmatum* 'Osakazuki'), prized for its vivid crimson leaves.

Late in the year, the white or pink flowers of the fall-blooming cherry, *Prunus subhirtella* 'Autumnalis,' look lovely when set in front of yews. Or surround a pencil-thin *Juniperus scopulorum* 'Skyrocket' with some winter- to spring-blooming heaths, perhaps with a white-barked quaking aspen *(Populus tremuloides)* or a red-barked *Prunus maackii.*

▲ **Spring companions** Almond blossom *(Prunus dulcis),* borne on leafless branches, weaves clouds of soft pink above early daffodils.

▼ **Summer canopy** The deciduous conifer dawn redwood *(Metasequoia glyptostroboides)* casts dappled shade over a summer underplanting of scarlet salvias and French marigolds growing between mounds of perennial blue *Festuca ovina* 'Glauca.'

▲ **Specimen planting** The Chinese whitebeam *(Sorbus hupehensis)* is an outstanding garden tree. It unfolds its sea-green ferny leaves in spring and bears clusters of white flowers in early summer. In the fall, the foliage turns yellow and red, creating a vivid contrast to its drooping bunches of red-stalked, white berries.

Such beauty is enhanced with an underplanting of barberries, whose arching branches are studded with coral-red fruits in fall. Some dwarf rhododendrons nestle below, surrounded by a glossy green carpet of *Cotoneaster dammeri* that provides year-round cover.

▶ **Woodland associates** The moist, shady soil beneath mature trees is a favored habitat for many types of ferns, including wood ferns *(Dryopteris* species), common polypody, and the hardy shield ferns *(Polystichum* species). Common ivy trails among the ferns, and dog violets *(Viola riviniana)* spread leafy ground cover that is adorned with pale violet blooms in spring.

◄ **Sea of blue** The Spanish bluebell *(Hyacinthoides hispanica)* thrives in light shade and naturalizes as far north as zone 5. Its spikes of clear blue bells make charming partners for the white, purple-stained goblets of *Magnolia* x *soulangiana,* which open at the same time as the poet's narcissus 'Actaea,' in late spring.

▼ **Leaf contrast** The fall colors of a Japanese maple *(Acer palmatum* 'Aka-shigitatsu-sawa') change from light green and red-tinted to fiery crimson and purple. A neighboring holly bush, a gold-and-green variegated cultivar of *Ilex aquifolium,* lends superb contrast in color and leaf form.

▲ **Bog lovers** The swamp cypress *(Taxodium distichum)* prospers in moist, boggy soil. It is clothed from late spring in bright green frondlike foliage that turns yellow and then bronze-red in the fall.
The happy companions in this large bed are astilbes, with their fluffy, pale pink flower plumes, as well as the large-leaved perennial *Rodgersia podophylla,* with its purple-tinted foliage.

11

▲ All things bright and beautiful A profusion of spring colors carpets the ground beneath the bare branches of a sycamore tree. Tall drumstick primroses *(Primula denticulata),* trumpet daffodils, and the checkered bells of *Fritillaria meleagris* are prominent in this floral underplanting. Lungwort *(Pulmonaria saccharata),* with its white-spotted leaves, spires of grape hyacinths *(Muscari),* and starry *Anemone blanda* display varied shades of blue. Clumps of low-growing *Primula vulgaris* bring splashes of yellow and pale green to the composition.

▲ In a Japanese garden A feeling of privacy and quiet contemplation is achieved with a congenial planting of Japanese maples, bamboos, and grasses. Strong variations in color and form are evident, from the filigree maple leaves of pale green and light purple to the dark green linear foliage topping the canes of *Pleioblastus humilis.* The grassy mounds of golden *Hakonechloa macra* 'Aureola,' planted in the foreground, add further contrast to the setting.

▶ Showers of gold The easily grown *Laburnum* x *watereri* 'Vossii' is gorgeous in early summer. It is remarkably free-flowering, with drooping trusses of golden blossoms that may be as long as 2 ft (60 cm). Here, they rain down over a naturalized group of ornamental onions *(Allium giganteum),* softening their bright rose-lilac flower globes.

Grouping trees

A few trees are particularly outstanding and are often best planted as individual specimens, so that nothing detracts from their beauty. The majority of garden trees, however, create a greater visual impact when they are planted in groups. Three European white birches, for example, look more attractive set in a group than when they are planted as lone trees. And if one variegated holly is set among other plain, dark green ones, it brightens the whole composition.

Group planting is not limited to the same kind of trees. If they have the same needs, evergreen trees mix well with deciduous types, providing interest when the others have lost their leaves.

In the winter, weeping trees are good companions for evergreens, the grace of their leafless branches bringing a touch of lightness to the somber greens.

One of the most beautiful springtime sights is a group of fruit trees in blossom. Instead of planting several of the same species together, try growing a mixture of ornamental cherries and flowering crab apples. That way you will be cheered by a haze of pinks and whites throughout an extended flowering season.

In summer, when the leaves of deciduous trees have unfurled, foliage color becomes important. Use a purple-leaved tree *(Acer platanoides* 'Crimson King' or *Prunus cerasifera* 'Nigra') or a golden-leaved one *(Gleditsia triacanthos inermis* 'Sunburst') to ornament a mostly green canopy. But be wary of too much purple foliage because it can have a dull, heavy effect.

For fall displays, keep in mind that not all trees have foliage that changes color dramatically. And among those that do, try not to plant any together whose colors clash. The leaves of poplars and birches turn yellow, for example, while those of *Sorbus* become orange and red.

In a small garden, there is often room for only one tree. Underplant it with bulbs, shrubs, and perennials that reflect or contrast with the tree's foliage to make a colorful, interesting composition.

▲ **Contrasting shapes** The waterfall effect of a weeping willow *(Salix caprea* 'Pendula') is emphasized by a variegated holly clipped into a formal pyramid shape. In front, the rounded form of a low-growing *Skimmia japonica* unifies the grouping.

▼ **Springtime display** *Magnolia* x *soulangiana*, with its large, white goblet-shaped flowers, and *Amelanchier lamarckii*, frothing with small white blossoms, support and nicely complement each other.

▶ **Cool corner** The magnificent golden leaves of an Indian bean tree *(Catalpa bignonioides* 'Aurea') appear almost translucent above an underplanting of yellow-flowered perennials — low-growing *Sedum reflexum* and silver-leaved *Senecio cineraria*. A nearby *Hydrangea quercifolia* adds a dash of white to the composition, though in the fall it will be transformed into a blaze of vivid foliage.

▼ **Sculptural forms** Two conifers create a stunning focal point in a large garden. The blue-white foliage and distinctive conical shape of *Picea pungens* 'Hoopsii' are thrown into sharp relief against the bright green of a *Chamaecyparis lawsoniana* cultivar. The conifers rise like noble spires from a base of feathery ferns.

▲ **Foliage contrast** The gold-green foliage of *Robinia pseudoacacia* 'Frisia' provides an airy contrast to the dense column of blue-gray *Cupressus arizonica* 'Pyramidalis.'

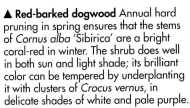

▼ **Perfumed wintersweet** A favorite of southern gardeners, wintersweet *(Chimonanthus praecox)* blooms in zones 8 and farther south in midwinter, overwhelming passersby with its honey-scented perfume. Adaptable to sun or partial shade, this shrub is easily transplanted and tolerates a wide range of soils as long as they are well drained. In zone 7 (the northern edge of its range), wintersweet should be set in a sheltered spot.

With its claw-shaped yellow blossoms, wintersweet is more odd in appearance than beautiful — in the winter its appearance will be enhanced if the bases of its 10 ft (3 m) tall naked branches are hidden by the evergreen foliage and plump flower buds of *Helleborus foetidus*, as well as by clumps of snowdrops.

▲ **Red-barked dogwood** Annual hard pruning in spring ensures that the stems of *Cornus alba* 'Sibirica' are a bright coral-red in winter. The shrub does well in both sun and light shade; its brilliant color can be tempered by underplanting it with clusters of *Crocus vernus*, in delicate shades of white and pale purple.

▲ **Paperbark maple** The main attraction of the Chinese paperbark maple *(Acer griseum)* is its cinnamon-colored bark that peels off in large flakes to reveal a fresh, glowing copper layer underneath. The horse-chestnut-like foliage of *Rodgersia podophylla* echoes the distinctive color theme.

▲ **Pussy willow** The weeping branches of *Salix caprea* 'Pendula' rain silvery catkins over an underplanting of wine-purple *Primula* 'Wanda Hybrids.' Clumps of old-fashioned pheasant's-eye narcissus *(Narcissus poeticus),* naturalized in the grassy glade, soften the vivid primrose color.

◄ **Spring trumpeters** The graceful, weeping silver birch *(Betula pendula* 'Youngii') is ideal for the smaller garden. Its ornamental bark and curtain of green leaves, which turn butter-yellow in the fall, can be truly appreciated when the tree is used as a lawn specimen. In the spring its natural companions are trumpet daffodils such as 'Golden Harvest.' Winter-flowering heathers effectively highlight the silvery bark.

CONIFER COMPANIONS

**With their beautiful forms and coloring,
conifers make attractive specimen trees that add
charm to a variety of garden plantings.**

Conifers may lack the showy blooms of flowering shrubs and trees, but they make up for this with their rich assortment of sizes, shapes, foliage textures, and colors. Fully hardy and easy to grow in a variety of soils, they are excellent for hedges. Yews in particular lend themselves superbly to topiary. Additionally, almost all conifers are evergreen.

Conifers can bring a bleak garden to life in winter and act as a calming backdrop to vibrant flower displays in summer. As background trees, they provide shelter and privacy.

You can create stunning effects by mixing conifers with different-colored foliage. For example, try planting a multihued hedge of green-and-golden false cypresses, or set them among broad-leaved trees and shrubs.

Many conifers are impressive in stature and make wonderful specimen trees on large lawns and in landscape designs. Conical and upright types are appropriate for the average-size garden, planted in groups of their own or as focal points among ornamental plants. They bring height and contrast to textures when planted in heather beds. Dwarf conifers are invaluable in the rock garden, and true miniatures flourish in container gardens and window boxes.

Conifers make good foliage foils and focal points in shrub and mixed borders. You can select the emerald green of *Thuja occidentalis*, the golden leaves of *Chamaecyparis lawsoniana* 'Stewartii,' the shrubby forms of dwarf firs (*Abies* species), the horizontal tiers of several junipers, or the powerful blue of the Colorado spruce (*Picea pungens* 'Glauca').

▲ **Winter cheer** A pair of Lawson cypresses *(Chamaecyparis lawsoniana* 'Kilmacurragh') stand tall and columnar above a carpet of pink *Erica carnea* 'Winter Beauty.' The dark green foliage responds well to clipping.

▼ **Mixed border** Dwarf forms of *Chamaecyparis lawsoniana* also have columnar lines and span a range of foliage colors — green, blue, gray, yellow, and variegated. These grow slowly and are good vertical accents in herbaceous and mixed shrub borders.

◄ **Shape contrasts** The slender *Juniperus scopulorum* 'Skyrocket' occupies little space and therefore works well in small gardens. Its pencil-slim form nicely offsets the rounded shapes of evergreen, glossy-leaved, and white-flowered Mexican orange *(Choisya ternata)* and pink-flowered *Daphne* x *burkwoodii* — both scented and in full bloom during the spring.

▼ **Golden accent** The Oriental arborvitae *(Platycladus orientalis)* has a formal habit, with its foliage held in dense vertical sprays. Here, a golden-leaved dwarf cultivar glows throughout the summer in the company of *Convolvulus althaeoides,* a mass of gray-green leaves and satiny-pink, funnel-shaped flowers. In the fall, this arborvitae develops bronze tints.

◀ **Gold companions** The Leyland cypress (x *Cupressocyparis leylandii)* is the fastest growing of all conifers, rising 3 ft (90 cm) a year. This tree is tolerant of pollution and suitable for all types of soil. It is also excellent for tall hedges and for windscreens, although in the latter capacity it is not recommended for small gardens.

The cultivar 'Castlewellan Gold' is slower growing than the species; its golden yellow foliage beautifully complements a variegated dogwood (*Cornus alba* 'Spaethii').

▶ **Conifer groups** A mixed planting of conifers, including blue spruces, golden-needled pines and chamaecyparises, and a gray-green juniper, is partnered by a carpet of heathers to provide an association with year-round interest. In the fall, the diverse shapes and colors are illuminated by the deep purple-red tints of *Amelanchier canadensis.*

▼ **Miniature conifers** Slow growing and rarely exceeding 2 ft (60 cm) in height, *Juniperus communis* 'Compressa' is ideal for rock gardens and container plantings. Its slim, upright branches are compressed into a tight columnar form, adding height to an alpine landscape. Here, two gray-green conifers give substance to a grouping of golden *Potentilla tabernaemontani,* blue *Aquilegia bertolonii,* and white-variegated *Arabis ferdinandi-coburgii* 'Variegata.'

◄ **Backdrop color** The rich green geometric outline of aromatic *Platycladus orientalis* offers a dramatic background for the large, clear pink blooms of the Gallica rose 'Complicata.' On early-summer days, the delicate scent from the roses blends with that of lavender at the base of the grouping.

► **Mountain pines** The dwarf stone pine *(Pinus pumila)* is ultrahardy (to zone 4) and well suited to a rock garden. Here, the cultivar 'Dwarf Blue' makes an arresting vertical accent above a ground cover of New Zealand burs *(Acaena anserinifolia)*, with insignificant flowers but outstanding blue-gray foliage and pinkish-brown burs.

▼ **Weeping cedar** The Atlas cedar *(Cedrus atlantica)* is a large, fast-growing conifer. However, its cultivar 'Glauca Pendula', is a superb small tree with pendulous branches thickly clothed with blue-green leaves. Here, it is a backdrop for a pool lined with blue and white irises.

CHOOSING TREES

The right choice of tree can enhance every garden, even the smallest plot, by adding height, impact, and perspective to it.

In order to achieve the distinctive appeal of maturity, a garden should contain at least one tree, but preferably two or three. Without trees, it is severely lacking in height and backbone. A tree can become a focal point — its size, shape, and color accenting a garden's good points and concealing its flaws.

You may decide not to plant any trees because you think they will take too long to grow. That would be a mistake. With careful selection, a tree can be found that suits every garden, however small or confined it may be. Although some trees take years to reach their mature shape, you can derive immeasurable pleasure from

watching a young one develop. Deciduous trees, for example, provide interesting color and form throughout the year — from the moment their swelling buds are succeeded by leaves, flowers, fruits, and fall tints, to their winter display of bare branches and attractive bark.

With their year-round foliage, evergreens — broad-leaved trees and conifers — come into their own in the winter, when they continue to bring life and color to the slumbering garden and offer shelter to the native bird population.

Do not be impatient, however, when you are shopping for trees, as this will cost you dearly. Keep in mind that young, and therefore

▲ **An easy match** Few trees are so easy to integrate into a garden as the kousa dogwood *(Cornus kousa)*. The blizzard of white flowers it bears in late spring is a perfect foil for colorful annual flowers.

▼ **Japanese angelica tree** This small ornamental tree *(Aralia elata 'Variegata')* bears arching foliage sprays with creamy white margins.

smaller, plants are much less expensive to buy than those grown on to a larger size in a nursery. In addition, they are easier to transplant and so experience less trauma than mature trees do.

In a small garden, some trees — even those that reach only 25 ft (7.5 m) in height — should be avoided, for they cast too much shade or dominate the space. Height and spread without excess weight are the most important considerations. Some of the maples and crab apples, with their rounded heads of lightweight foliage, are ideal for the smaller plot and rarely outgrow their allotted space.

Also, it is a good idea to learn about the root systems of the trees that interest you. Unfortunately, certain types can create major problems. Willows, for instance, have long roots that, in their search for water and nutrients, can penetrate and extensively damage drains. In addition, the roots of large trees planted too close to buildings and walls can severely affect the foundations. In clay soils, particularly during prolonged drought, the amount of water taken up by trees can cause subsidence.

▶ **Weeping European birch** Ideal for the small garden, *Betula pendula* 'Youngii' trails its slender branches and pale green foliage as a backdrop for spring daffodils and early tulips.

Tree characteristics
Before purchasing a tree, you must take into account its ultimate height, the spread of the branches, and the quality of its foliage. At the same time, consider the tree's winter hardiness and

▲ **Shade trees** Mature trees lightly shade a glorious mixture of vivid blue and soft yellow plants. Tall *Meconopsis betonicifolia* towers impressively above eye-catching *Primula florindae* and handsome *Hosta sieboldiana*.

▲ **Golden rain** Laden with cascading sprays of yellow pea flowers in late spring and early summer, the golden rain tree *(Laburnum)* is a spectacular sight. It is a popular choice for small gardens, although parts of the tree, especially the seeds, are poisonous.

its final planting site, its soil, position, and exposure to wind. Then, once you have made a selection, the next step is to provide the tree with the best possible growing conditions so that it will flourish.

While it is best to plant deciduous trees in the spring or fall during their dormant season, container-grown trees can be set out at almost any time. All types require fertile soil and plenty of water in their early years until they have established a good root system. In addition, they should be firmly staked and secured with proper tree ties.

Tree shapes

Trees come in many shapes and sizes, so carefully choose ones that are appropriate for your garden, especially if space is at a premium. To add height without smothering other plants, select slender, upright species. For a more relaxed effect, a tree of spreading habit may be preferable. Although low branches block access in a confined area and can be a nuisance at transplanting time, they provide welcome shade, particularly for woodland plants. Since young trees rarely reflect their eventual mature shape, discuss their development with the nursery before buying.

Upright shapes The strong vertical accent of a tall, green column works well in some gardens, but looks too abrupt and formal in others. The upright cultivars of many popular trees, such as the

Japanese cherry *Prunus serrulata* 'Amanogawa' or the crab apple *Malus tschonoskii*, are eminently suitable for the small garden, because their neat pattern of growth creates little shade and does not take up too much space.

Weeping shapes Pendulous trees have become fashionable in small gardens, where their controlled outlines are quite effective. Try to avoid the weeping willow *(Salix alba* 'Tristis') despite its beauty as a young tree. It is easy to forget how thirsty these roots are and how much space it requires. The willow-leaved pear *(Pyrus salicifolia* 'Pendula'), a small weeping tree with creamy blossoms and silvery foliage, is a much better choice.

The ornamental cherry *Prunus subhirtella* 'Pendula' is another fine possibility for the small garden. Its clusters of pink spring flowers are followed by dense

23

drooping leaves that turn brilliant yellow in the fall.

The graceful growth habit of the European white birch *(Betula pendula),* with its light and airy foliage, makes this tree a good candidate for planting individually as a specimen or in a group. The cultivar 'Youngii' remains compact and so is a lovely dome-shaped tree for a small garden.

Round shapes If you have room for only a single tree, you may prefer one with a simple round crown. An outstanding example is the English hawthorn *(Crataegus laevigata).* The many cultivars of this handsome tree bear clusters of flowers that are either white, red, or a shade of pink, followed by glossy red or yellow fruits. The sharp thorns of this species, how-ever, make it a poor choice for areas where children play.

The maple family includes many trees with pleasant rounded shapes. The sycamore *(Acer pseudoplatanus* 'Brilliantissimum') is a striking example. Its curved outline is highlighted by the coral-pink of its young foliage, which turns pale green as it matures. The sweet gum tree *(Liquidambar styraciflua),* often mistaken for a maple, is conical when young; in maturity the tree develops a domed crown. It is lovely in the fall, when the maple-like green leaves turn orange, red, or purple. The staghorn sumac *(Rhus typhina),* with its velvety bark and pendulous shape, also has vibrant foliage in the fall.

Colored foliage

Trees with strikingly colored foliage, such as the purple and orange members of the *Acer* family, make good specimen plantings. Among the golden-leaved trees that look spectacular on their own in the garden are the false acacia *(Robinia pseudoacacia* 'Frisia') and the Indian bean tree *(Catalpa bignonioides* 'Aurea'), whose young foliage is coppery.

For variegated leaf color, pick the small Japanese angelica tree *(Aralia elata* 'Variegata'), which is grown for its handsome, large pinnate leaves that have wide, creamy white margins.

To create a truly dramatic effect, plant the copper beech *(Fagus sylvatica* 'Atropunicea') in your garden — it bears leaves in various shades of purplish-red, ranging from a light hue to a magnificent deep, intense copper.

Flowering trees

Many in the almond and cherry *(Prunus)* group are exquisite flowering trees, especially the ornamental Higan cherry *(P. subhirtella),* with its stunning profusion of spring blooms.

A good choice for medium-size gardens from zones 5 to 7 is the popular laburnum, or golden rain tree *(Laburnum × watereri* 'Vossii'). In late spring and early summer it displays drooping golden blooms. However, it is poisonous — especially the seeds — and unsuitable for gardens where young children are present.

Of all the flowering trees, few can rival the magnolias. Some are

▲ **Sweet gum tree** Notable for its vibrant fall colors, the slender, pyramidal sweet gum *(Liquidambar styraciflua)* is usually adorned with glossy, dark green maplelike leaves.

◀ **Japanese maple** The slow-growing and spreading *Acer japonicum* 'Aureum' is splendid for small gardens. It does best in light shade, where its golden yellow foliage cannot be scorched by too much sunlight. The Japanese maple tolerates alkaline soils.

▲ Deciduous azaleas
Attaining almost treelike stature, deciduous azaleas flower in late spring and make magnificent specimen plants for small gardens. They also associate well with bluebells. In fall their foliage develops red and golden tints, which can be reflected in an underplanting of goblet-shaped colchicums.

◄ Winter cheer The ground beneath the bare branches of deciduous trees is a perfect spot for small late-winter and early-spring flowering bulbs. Winter aconites (*Eranthis hyemalis*), with their green rufflike collars and golden flower globes, appear among the lilac early-spring *Crocus tomasinianus.* Dainty pink *Cyclamen coum* accompanies these pastel-colored plants.

expansive, and thus require plenty of room, but the lovely, slow-growing *Magnolia stellata* fits into most gardening schemes.

Many fruit-bearing plants provide a superb flowering display that is succeeded by attractive fruits. The crab apples *(Malus* species), for example, offer clouds of white, pink, or red flowers in spring, followed by orange, golden, or scarlet fruits that may stay on the trees into winter.

The mountain ashes *(Sorbus* species and cultivars) have a long flowering season and an extended display of brilliantly colored fruits. Some species, such as *S. aucuparia* 'Beissneri,' also have striking fall foliage.

Evergreen trees
If you want year-round foliage, consider holly *(Ilex* species and cultivars), especially those with leaves that have splashes or margins of silver or gold. A slow-growing tree, holly can be easily trimmed to a manageable height.

The Australian eucalyptuses *(Eucalyptus* species), or gum trees, are very popular in frost-free regions. Their rather sparse foliage does not cast dense shade, and thus will not stifle under-plantings. Best adapted to the arid warmth of the West Coast, eucalyptuses grow so well in southern California that they may be regarded as an invasive pest. Grown as a specimen plant, the red-flowering gum *(E. ficifolia)* develops into a rough-barked tree, 30-50 ft (9-15 m) tall, that covers itself with clusters of red to pink flowers in midsummer. The snow gum *(E. niphophila),* a slow-growing species with beautiful mottled bark and large, leathery gray-green leaves, is the hardiest species (to zone 8) of all. The cider gum *(E. gunnii)* is often cut back each year to the size of a shrub. Its attractive, blue-green or silvery white foliage is prized by flower arrangers. Left un-pruned, it grows very quickly into a spear-shaped tree, growing by 3-6 ft (90-180 cm) a year.

The strawberry tree *(Arbutus unedo),* a handsome evergreen with urn-shaped white or pink fall flowers and orange-red strawberrylike fruits, grows slowly and is perfect for small gardens.

Conifers
In maturity, many conifers grow to the size of forest trees and are unsuitable for small gardens. Those with columnar shapes, however, such as *Chamaecyparis lawsoniana* 'Columnaris,' *Juniperus communis* 'Hibernica,' or the golden Irish yew *(Taxus baccata* 'Fastigiata Aurea'), make marvelous specimen trees.

Dwarf conifers, the mainstay of many small gardens, come in a wide range of shapes and colors, and are often planted either among heathers in the rock garden or individually, as part of a lawn grouping.

▼ **Fruit trees** Shade-loving plants, such as blue and white willow bellflowers *(Campanula persicifolia)* and red and purple foxgloves, help turn a mature apple tree into a stunning focal point.

◄ **Snow gum tree** Most evergreens cast dense permanent shade that makes it impossible for anything to grow beneath them. The eucalyptuses, or gum trees, however, are generally well branched with long, narrow leaves that allow light to filter through.

The fast-growing snow gum *(Eucalyptus niphophila)* is the hardiest species, weathering frosts better than it does strong winds. Cool colors complement its near-white trunk, and suitable companions include ground-covering dead nettle *(Lamium maculatum* 'Beacon Silver'), with its neat, silvery evergreen leaves, and the shrubby *Euphorbia characias,* which produces clusters of gray-green dense foliage. In early spring, its pale yellow flower bracts add a bright splash to the grouping.

► **Laburnum tunnel** Many formal Old World gardens feature a laburnum walk comprised of trees that are pleached and trained to form a tunnel of foliage — a cool vantage point from which to view the garden during hot weather. When the trees bloom in late spring and early summer, the walk seems to cascade with golden yellow blooms.

The effect is spectacular, especially in association with an underplanting of rose-purple ornamental onions *(Allium rosenbachianum)* that flower at the same time. Such pleasing partnerships, on a smaller scale, can easily be achieved in more modest gardens.

▶ **Star magnolia** The slow-growing *Magnolia stellata* begins to flower while still very young, opening its fragrant white blossoms to form wide stars in midspring. The many-petaled blooms have faint traces of purple at their base — a color theme picked up in an underplanting of bergenias. The glossy green foliage of this clump-forming perennial thrives in shade cast by the magnolia's summer canopy.

▼ **Floral carpet** Little *Cyclamen hederifolium* flourishes on the West Coast and in the East as far north as zone 7, in protected spots with rich soil. Preferring the moist shade found beneath deciduous trees and shrubs, this bulb bears mauve, pink, and white flowers from late summer through fall, amid dark green, silver-marbled leaves.

FALL COLORS

With careful planning and planting, a glorious fall show of leaves and berries can follow summer flowers.

Fall is one of the most beautiful times of the year. The dying leaves of deciduous trees and shrubs blaze with color, and fruits and berries add brilliant hues of red, yellow, orange, purple, and white to the scene. With a wide range of cultivated plants to choose from, it is easy to plan your garden so that summer's vivid flowers are followed by a dazzling fall display.

Only in the largest gardens can a whole area be devoted solely to a fall show. For average and small gardens, choose compact plants that are attractive for weeks or even months, rather than brief spells. Try to blend those that look spectacular in fall with plants that are outstanding in flower or foliage at other times of the year.

When choosing a plant, weigh its fall appearance against the way it looks during the rest of the year. Some, such as serviceberry *(Amelanchier canadensis),* deciduous azaleas *(Rhododendron),* ornamental cherries *(Prunus),* and crab apples *(Malus)* have attractive spring flowers as well as striking fall foliage or berries (or both). Others, such as *Parrotia persica,* are relatively dull except for their extremely brief fall show. And some, such as *Liquidambar, Ginkgo,* and tulip tree *(Liriodendron),* are beautiful but too large for the average garden.

Every type of plant — from trees, shrubs, and climbers to perennials, biennials (such as pansies), annuals (in zones 9-11, fall is the best season to plant many of these), and bulbs — can be represented in the fall garden. Most people carefully organize their fall garden to obtain a good balance of colorful flowers, foliage, and fruit or berries.

Leaves
You only have to cast your eye across a hillside covered with birches, aspens, or maples to know that fall leaf color is the most dramatic visual aspect of the season. Equally beautiful displays of fall foliage can be created in the garden. Virtually all the maples, many deciduous berberises, viburnums, cotoneasters, smoke bush *(Cotinus),* dogwoods *(Cornus),* ornamental blueberries *(Vaccinium),* and various species of *Parthenocissus* are recommended. If space permits, include plants that will give a range of colors. For yellow, there's birch or beech; for vivid reds *Euonymus alata* 'Compactus,' *Berberis thunbergii,* or *Acer palmatum;* and for orange the brilliantly colored sumac *(Rhus typhina)* or *Fothergilla major.*

As leaf fall is inevitably followed by bare branches, consider as well the shape and bark color of a given deciduous tree or shrub. Those with an attractive winter presence, such as birches, sumacs, several of the shrubby

▲ **Fall cones** Although cones are not as striking as fruits and foliage, they are a valuable feature of the fall scene. Cones vary in shape, size, and texture, and their subtle colors are welcome in any display.

▼ **Foliage colors** Red, orange, gold, russet, and yellow are all present in this dramatic fall display. Color is affected by climatic variations: a hot, dry summer or a warm and cloudy fall often results in dull leaf colors.

willows, and some dogwoods and maples, are well worth including in a planting scheme.

Berries, fruit, and seedpods
Apart from foliage, fruit is the other major source of fall color. A vast color range is available, and some plants offer massive clusters of berries that far outshine the leaves and stems. Cotoneasters and pyracanthas — with red, orange, or yellow berries — are very popular. Other options are the translucent red berries of the European cranberry *(Viburnum opulus)*, set off to perfection by bright yellow fall leaves or the red, orange, white, or pink berry clusters of the various kinds of mountain ash *(Sorbus)*.

Most crab apples and flowering quinces have an attractive shape as well as interesting foliage, flowers, and fruit. Chinese lanterns *(Physalis alkekengi)*, however, despite their intriguing fruits, have insignificant flowers, dull foliage, and a sprawling, invasive growth habit.

Specialist rose nurseries stock a diverse range of old-fashioned shrub roses with hips in many different shapes and colors. There are roses with huge round hips, flask-shaped hips, hips carried in sprays or clusters, and hips ranging in color from clear orange to deepest crimson and even black.

Conifer cones — usually more subtly colored than flowers, fruit, and foliage — also add interest. Sizes vary from the huge cones of California's Coulter pine, which may measure 14 in (35 cm) long, to the delicate flowerlike cones of larch; colors range from the pinkish red of *Picea likiangensis* to the blue-black of *Abies forrestii*.

The seed heads of silky yellow-flowered *Clematis tangutica* and *C. orientalis*, and the old-fashioned silver circles of honesty, offer subtle fall tones. And a large clump of pampas grass makes an effective fall focal point on a lawn.

Consider how long a plant will put on a good fall show. Delicate seedpods are vulnerable to storms, and brilliantly colored fall leaves, such as those of burning bush *(Euonymus alata)*, may last only a few days. Fruits, too, vary widely in their persistence: the crab apple 'Centurion' holds its

▲ **Pool reflections** Richly colored fall foliage is dramatically mirrored in the still waters of a pool. In the garden trees and shrubs should be sited a good distance from pools, so that their leaves do not dirty the water and clog fountain pumps.

▲ ▶ **Seedpods** The spindle tree *(Euonymus europaeus)* is weighed down in fall with clusters of seedpods — those of the cultivar 'Red Cascade' are rosy red.

▶ **Ornamental vine** *Parthenocissus henryana,* silver-vein creeper, embroiders a wall with its colorful foliage. Silver and green in summer, the leaves turn scarlet in fall.

▲ **Japanese maples** The rounded form and divided leaves of Japanese maple *(Acer palmatum* 'Dissectum') are most distinctive in fall, when clothed in hues of yellow, orange, and red.

cherry-red fruits for several months, while those of 'Cotton Candy' drop soon after ripening.

Ornamental fruit color

Most ornamental fruits and berries are in the orange-red range. The colors vary in intensity, from bright and luminous to deeper and less eye-catching hues. As a rule, a background of paler or darker foliage helps them to stand out more than a green of the same intensity.

Dark blue, dark purple, or black ornamental fruits can be beautiful when viewed close up and are excellent for flower arranging. Generally, however, dark fruits have little impact when seen from a distance. Dark fruits with a pale, waxy bloom, such as those of mahonia and some berberises, appear more prominent when they are seen against deep green foliage.

White or light-colored berries can be eye-catching, especially when they are placed against a

contrasting backdrop. For example, the pale fruit produced by snowberries *(Symphoricarpos albus)* is particularly striking when seen against a somber yew hedge.

Unripe green berries tend to blend with the surrounding greenery. They have much more impact when they are set against red, purple, or yellow foliage.

Fruiting partners

The fall foliage of some plants creates a perfect setting for their own fruits or pods — for example, rock cotoneaster *(Cotoneaster horizontalis)* has crimson fall foliage and scarlet berries.

Evergreen and semievergreen plants provide their own foliage backdrop. However, deciduous fruiting plants that retain their

▼ **Rose hips** The arching branches of *Rosa moyesii* 'Geranium' are attractively adorned with bright red flowers in midsummer. The fall display of drooping, flask-shaped crimson hips is equally spectacular.

bounty after their leaves have fallen need carefully chosen partners. For example, the bright red berry spikes of Italian arum *(Arum italicum)* look more effective rising out of a ground cover of ivy or vinca than emerging from dead leaves or bare earth.

Try to avoid potential clashes when an ornamental fruiting plant is trained up or displayed against a wall. Orange and red berries can clash with red brickwork, especially if it is new, but they will often look attractive set against mellow or pale brickwork, stucco, or natural stone. They also look good against dark or light wooden fences.

Yellow and white berries are best set against dark brickwork, stone, or wood; they tend to blend in with pale backgrounds and so disappear from view.

Set plants with ornamental fruits where they can be seen from house windows. Plants can be trained to hang over certain windows, so that their fruit-laden branches frame the outward view.

Fruiting plants are also effective when planted near paths and patios, and can make a pretty framework for the entrance to a garden, porch, or front door.

Some low-growing evergreen fruiting plants, such as the bearberries *(Arctostaphylos* species), make excellent ground covers. Try pernettyas and butcher's-broom in a mixed border or wild garden.

▲ **Pure honesty** The oval seedpods of honesty *(Lunaria annua)* are so transparent that the seeds show through them. For dried flower bouquets, peel off the outer covering and remove the black seeds.

▶ **Crab apples** Resplendent in late spring, crab apples *(Malus* species) bear massed clusters of single or double, white, pink, or red flowers. They reach a second high point in fall, when their branches are laden with fruit. These fruits range in size from ¼-2 in (½-5 cm) in diameter, depending on the cultivar, and may ripen to yellow, pink, orange, or red. Some crab apples retain their fruit almost until spring.

◀ **Chinese lanterns** The bright orange seedpods of *Physalis alkekengi* are wonderfully long-lasting in dried flower arrangements. However, in leaf and flower, these hardy perennials have little ornamental value, and they are extremely invasive and self-seeding.

▲ **European cranberry** *(Viburnum opulus* 'Compactum') is a wide-spreading deciduous shrub with maplelike leaves and white flower heads in summer. In fall it bears long-lasting bright red berries.

▼ **Blue barberry** The evergreen *Berberis darwinii,* with its glossy hollylike foliage, is outstanding throughout the year. In late spring it bears clusters of rich yellow flowers, followed in fall by waxy blue berries.

▼ **Mountain ash** A Chinese relative of the American mountain ash, *Sorbus hupehensis* is an elegant small tree with blue-green leaves that turn brilliant orange in fall. Drooping clusters of white berries develop in late summer.

Plants with pendent ornamental fruit, such as Himalayan honeysuckle *(Leycesteria formosa)* and ornamental grapes, are ideally sited where they can be viewed from below. Ornamental grapes can be trained over a pergola situated over a patio or path, and *Leycesteria formosa* looks effective grown in a raised bed.

Pollinating partners

The natural function of berry color is to attract birds, which then eat the berries and distribute the seed, thus increasing the species' chance of survival. Birds' tastes vary, and locality, availability of other nearby food, and weather conditions also affect which berries get eaten. Berries of certain plants, such as skimmia and ivy, are often left alone. Others, such as those of dogwood, tend to disappear immediately.

Some plants, such as sea buckthorn, skimmia, butcher's-broom, aucuba, and many hollies, are either male or female. Approximately one male plant is needed to pollinate three females and thereby ensure crops of berries. Garden centers should specify the sex of plants where relevant, so check labels carefully.

Some plants, such as laurustinus and arbutus, only fruit in

▲ **Red-stemmed dogwood** The easily grown *Cornus alba* 'Sibirica,' with its bright red stems, looks striking in the company of *Euonymus fortunei* 'Emerald 'n' Gold,' which is tinged with pink as winter approaches.

▼ **Fire thorn** The evergreen *Pyracantha* grows well in a wide range of soils and sites. Its creamy flowers in early summer are followed by clusters of berries; yellow-berried forms retain their fruits better than red-berried types.

◀ **Shades of red** The spindle tree *Euonymus europaeus* 'Red Cascade' provides a range of red hues in fall. As the green foliage turns purplish red, the crimson seedpods split open to reveal glossy orange fruits.

▼ **Stinking iris** Its pale purple summer flowers are insignificant and marred by a rank smell emitted from its evergreen leaves, but *Iris foetidissima* redeems itself in fall, when the large green pods peel back to display rows of orange-scarlet seeds. The fruiting stems are excellent for dried flower arrangements.

extremely favorable conditions. Many conifers and some broad-leaved trees, such as magnolias, produce cones and fruits only when they are mature. Dwarf conifers rarely bear cones.

Many plants fruit on young wood, and a severe pruning may remove the following year's display. This often occurs with mature wall-climbing pyracanthas, but a poor display one year is often made up for by excellent shows in following years.

Evergreen standbys

Evergreens, whether they are broad-leaved like elaeagnus or coniferous like yews and junipers, are as important in fall as they are in winter. Some of the smaller conifers — for example, *Juniperus horizontalis* — take on bronze, purplish, or red coloring in colder weather, thus adding valuable fall and winter interest.

There are also conifer cones that add subtle interest to the garden in winter. They range from the huge, upright cones of the noble fir to the delicate cones of larch and cryptomeria. Most cones develop from green to brown or silvery gray, but there are also white, orange, blue, violet, and nearly black varieties. Some cones will remain on the tree for at least a year or more before they fall.

Don't forget evergreen perennials, such as Christmas rose *(Helleborus niger),* and trailers, such as *Euonymus fortunei* 'Coloratus,' whose dark green leaves take on rich red tones in fall. Even the common ivy may have hints of red in cold weather.

Using fall color

Brilliant fall colors contrast well against a light or dark background, such as a whitewashed garden wall or a yew hedge. Select background settings carefully: a crimson Japanese maple seen against red brickwork or a yellow field maple *(Acer campestre)* set against ocher-yellow bricks looks garish.

However, a joy of fall planting is that there is room to experiment. Try using plants with eye-catching foliage as focal points, setting them in appropriate spots within beds and borders or break up fall color into paintlike dabs — set the tiny ivy-leaved cyclamen in pink drifts under a tree. Or use color as an exclamation point by placing a magnificent specimen tulip tree or clump of maples on a lawn. Virginia creeper *(Parthenocissus)* can be trained to cover a house for a breathtaking effect.

Shrub partners

Shrubs set the stage for every garden, creating a permanent backdrop for ever-changing groups of bulbs, herbaceous perennials, and annuals. During the year their floral displays, foliage tints, and berry colors alter with the seasons.

Many shrubs are chosen for their flowering qualities, but it can be a mistake to judge a shrub solely on the short time it is in bloom. Foliage can be of greater importance, as it is present for many months. Leaves come in a variety of shades — not only green, but also silver, gray, gold, and purple. Leaf size and texture range from the minuscule foliage of brooms to the huge fronds of fatsias, and from the leathery leaves of rhododendrons to the finely cut foliage of potentillas.

Some shrubs look superb in isolation, while others are best integrated in mixed borders with other shrubs or perennials. You can create many different combinations that harmonize in color and contrast pleasingly in form. With careful selection, a group of plants can maintain interest for months if their flowering displays overlap. Fall offers fresh delights with seasonal leaf colors and fruit.

Climbing shrubs are invaluable for clothing walls and fences with greenery and flowers and for extending the garden from the horizontal to the vertical plane. Clematises and roses make charming companions, and ivy is a particularly useful partner for more flamboyant but temporary climbers.

Roses, with their rich colors and diversity of form, are particular garden favorites. Although sometimes grown in beds of their own, they are truly outstanding in mixed borders or as specimen shrubs. They thrive in the company of delphiniums and lilies or lavenders and irises. They also flower prolifically in pots and patio beds and eagerly clamber up walls and trellises.

Shrub companions *Lavatera olbia* and purple *Buddleia davidii* create a spectacular long-flowering combination.

SHRUB HARMONY

Shrubs play an important role in the garden, offering strong support to other types of plants.

In most gardens today, it is the shrubs that give structure to the landscape. Whether planted in formal hedges, informal masses, or singly, shrubs lend height, weight, and substance to other plantings and provide interest throughout the year. Shrubs can be used as specimens, as background, or as focal points in mixed beds and borders, but group them to bring out the best from their varying colors and forms.

Although shrubs are usually chosen for their floral displays, these often last for only a relatively short time; the foliage lasts much longer. In some deciduous shrubs, the unfolding of the leaves in spring and their rich color in fall paint pictures of particular beauty. In addition, foliages offer varied compositions of green in summer.

Even more striking are shrubs with variegated leaves in shades of pink, gray, silver, and yellow, as well as ones with colored foliage, from the purple smoke trees to the golden *Lonicera nitida* 'Baggesen's Gold,' the gray-leaved hebes, and the silvery senecios.

Evergreens do not go through seasonal color changes, but they

▲ **Cool colors** Pure white, orange-scented flowers of *Philadelphus coronarius* and yellow lupinelike spires of *Thermopsis montana* rise from a sea of ice-blue *Veronica latifolia*.

▼ **Shades of pink** The purple-leaved smoke tree *(Cotinus coggygria* 'Purpureus') makes a dramatic background for purple-pink *Rodgersia pinnata* and pink *Astrantia maxima*.

◀ **Woodland associates** In cool, moist soil and dappled shade, woodland shrubs such as rhododendrons and azaleas burst into riotous color during late spring and early summer. Here, the fiery orange-red trumpets of an azalea are tempered by the cool yellow globes of a hybrid *Trollius*.

▼ **Evergreen gold** The hardy Asian spindle tree *(Euonymus fortunei* 'Emerald 'n' Gold') shines like a beacon on the cloudiest day. It forms a dense dwarf shrub, which glows next to the somber color of *Chamaecyparis* — especially in winter, when the gold-and-cream foliage takes on pinkish tones. In midsummer, blue and white *Viola cornuta*, fringed pinks, and white-flowered *Geranium pratense* 'Kashmir White' add their cottage-garden charm.

◀ **Beauty bush** Aptly named, the deciduous *Kolkwitzia amabilis* resembles a rippling fountain in early summer, when profuse porcelain-pink flowers decorate its arching branches. Such beauty needs little embellishment, but a foreground of upright foxgloves *(Digitalis purpurea)* is a perfect complement in color and shape. In fall the shrub's reddish leaves could be teamed with autumn crocus *(Colchicum speciosum)*.

display rich diversity in leaf form, ranging from the huge fanlike leaves of fatsias to the needlelike sprays of heathers and the tiny leaves of various cotoneasters and berberises. They add both life and color to the winter garden, and several cultivars delight the eye with their colorful clusters of berries and fruit.

Choosing shrubs

Flower color is likely to be one of the main criteria for choosing one particular shrub rather than another. Because of their tremendous diversity, shrubs offer some species in bloom during any season that the ground is not frozen hard, from the witch hazels *(Hamamelis* species) that blossom during winter thaws, to the ericas of late fall and very early spring, and the camellias that are in full bloom at Christmastime in the South.

However, even when flower color is the primary consideration, some thought should be given to a shrub's overall appearance and performance. Forsythia, for example, is one of our brightest and best-loved spring shrubs, but once its golden flowers have finished, it holds little attraction, with nondescript leaves and a tendency to grow leggy and gaunt unless the branches are pruned back hard every year.

Such shrubs should be sited in a spot where their blossoms can be enjoyed in full while their forms are hidden by other, more interesting companions during the remainder of the year.

As a rule, garden shrubs should be an equal mixture of deciduous and evergreen varieties, with a proportion of conifers and shrubs with colored foliage for contrast.

Grouping shrubs

Some shrubs are so outstanding in flower, leaf, and form that they deserve a prominent position, where they can be enjoyed all year. A typical example is the shrubby maple, especially a Japanese type like *Acer japonicum* 'Aureum,' with its deeply lobed, broad yellow leaves that turn brilliant red and orange in fall. Another example is the weeping butterfly bush *(Buddleia alternifolia)*, whose slender branches arch gracefully into a rippling, sweet-scented fountain of flowers in early summer.

Other shrubs have a much greater impact when planted in groups of three — the variegated elaeagnus, for example, with its gold-splashed evergreen leaves, is visually more impressive when planted in a group in a mixed border than if it is dotted about

▼ **The acid lovers** Given acid soil, light shade, and protection from strong winds, a shrubbery of mixed rhododendrons and azaleas is a stunning sight in late spring. Although available in a wide range of colors, these shrubs look most spectacular when colors and shapes are chosen with restraint.

▲ **Signs of spring** The ubiquitous but indispensable forsythia is the earliest of the spring-flowering shrubs, bursting into a mass of golden yellow blooms before the first leaf has unfolded. It is accompanied here by the dainty, clear pink blossoms of flowering cherry *(Prunus sargentii)*. At ground level a sprawling Japanese quince *(Chaenomeles* x *superba* 'Crimson and Gold') adds color to the spring scene.

◄ **Pink on pink** The climbing *Actinidia kolomikta* bears lightly scented white flowers in early summer. The shrub, however, is more remarkable for the tricolored leaf variegations found on the mature plant, where the top half of each leaf is creamy white flushed with pink. It forms a spectacular backdrop for the rich pink semidouble flowers of the rugosa rose 'Roseraie de l'Hay.'

▶ **The litmus test** Cultivars of mop-headed hydrangea *(Hydrangea macrophylla)* bloom pink or red in alkaline soils, but turn blue if treated regularly with acid fertilizer. Blooming from June through August (depending on the local climate), mop-headed hydrangeas are hardy from zone 6 to 9. Here, in alkaline soil, a cultivar with deep rose blossoms looks magnificent against a background of the old-fashioned rambler rose 'Dorothy Perkins,' whose tall stems are weighed down with festoons of blush-pink double blooms.

▼ **Wall protection** The common myrtle *(Myrtus communis),* so prolific in Mediterranean regions, is not reliably hardy north of zone 9, and grows best in the dry heat of the southern Pacific Coast. In favorable circumstances, however, the evergreen shrub will form a mound of dark green, glossy, and aromatic leaves, decorated in summer with fragrant white flowers with starlike golden stamens.

Myrtle looks best when partnered with other evergreen shrubs that thrive in the same sheltered conditions. In front is a dark green leathery-leaved *Pittosporum tobira,* whose fragrant white flowers mature through cream to butter-yellow. Sprawling in the foreground, clumps of a silver-leaved senecio add their bright yellow daisy flowers.

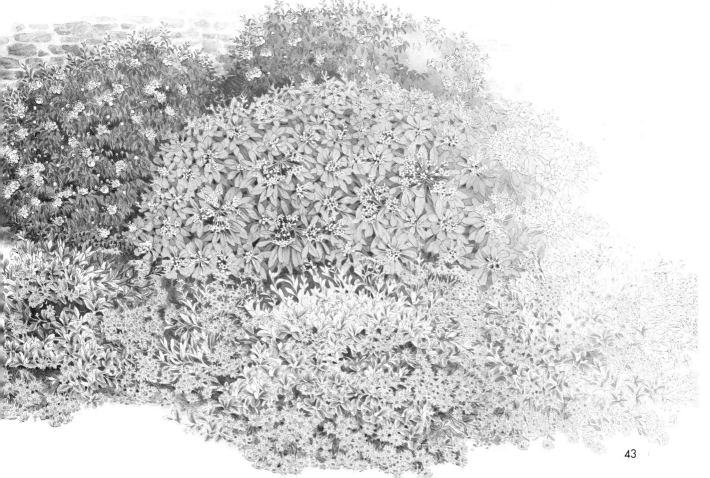

43

▲ **Summer snow** The popular snowball bush (*Viburnum opulus* 'Roseum,' also listed as 'Sterile') is adorned in late spring and early summer with creamy white "snowballs." These are striking among the dark green maplelike leaves, which later offer rich fall color. The shrub's solidity is lightened by the airy gracefulness of a tamarisk (*Tamarix parviflora),* whose branches are clothed with fluffy plumes of deep pink flowers.

◀ **Gray and silver** Foliage shrubs are invaluable as foils for strong flower colors. Here, gray-leaved lavender (*Lavandula angustifolia* 'Hidcote') and silvery *Artemisia absinthium* 'Lambrook Silver' flank an old-fashioned Gallica rose, 'Rosa Mundi' with its striking crimson-and-white striped blooms. Clumps of silvery gray-leaved, white-flowered *Dianthus* 'Mrs. Sinkins' create a perfect balance.

singly. Shrubs with strongly colored foliage, such as the purple smoke tree, can be overwhelming on their own, but when partnered by low-growing gray- or silver-leaved foliage plants, the overall effect is subdued and a picture of deliberate harmony is achieved.

In the same way, you can partner shrubs of contrasting outline or leaf form so that one highlights the other. For example, you can front narrowly upright shrubs, such as the deciduous *Stranvaesia davidiana,* with a mound of evergreen *Viburnum davidii;* arching tamarisk with neat hebes; and shrubby conifers with a carpet of heathers.

Shrub companions
Teaming shrubs with perennials, early- or late-flowering bulbs, ground covers, and summer annuals adds to the elegance of the shrubs in flower and prolongs the season of interest.

Choose companion plants whose colors harmonize or contrast with those of the shrubs. Alternatively, select plants whose handsome, long-lasting foliage will draw attention away from the nondescript leaves of some shrubs and will also effectively hide any unattractive bareness around their feet.

Create spring scenes by planting clumps of naturalized narcissi underneath snowy serviceberry *(Amelanchier* species), so that the shrub's dainty white flowers will shimmer above the golden trumpets. Another option is to match the shrub's blossoms with the drooping catkins of the corkscrew hazel, with its curiously twisted twigs and foliage. In addition, you could plant golden crocus or miniature blue irises at its feet.

Spring bulbs, too, are ideal for planting beneath deciduous shrubs grown for their vividly colored bare winter stems. You can plant white- or blue-striped crocuses, snowdrops, or golden winter aconites at the base of a red-stemmed dogwood *(Cornus alba* 'Sibirica') or a black-stemmed willow *(Salix gracilistyla* 'Melanostachys').

Stunning partnerships can be created when the flowering seasons of two shrubs overlap. Such associations work best when the flowers are within the same color range. To establish a long-lasting golden group, for example, plant a creamy yellow Warminster broom *(Cytisus × praecox)* next to

▲ **Silver foil** The tender shrub *Tanacetum ptarmaciflorum* is usually grown as a half-hardy annual. Its finely fretted silvery leaves make a beautiful foil for the scarlet-and-purple bells of this hardy (to zone 7) fuchsia cultivar.

▼ **Fuchsia theme** The graceful variegated *Fuchsia magellanica* 'Variegata' offers strong contrast for the bold foliage and stiff flower spikes of *Eucomis bicolor.*

a white-flowered currant *(Ribes sanguineum).* The broom comes into blossom as the currant begins to fade, thus extending the flowering display by two or three months. Alternatively, partner the butter-yellow blossoms of *Kerria japonica,* a graceful 5 ft (1.5 m) tall shrub, with the dainty white flowers of bridal-wreath *(Spiraea × arguta).*

The magnificent rhododendrons are mainly regarded as specimen shrubs and woodland plants, but the smaller hybrid azaleas can be successfully integrated in mixed borders. The Kurume group is particularly suitable: these dwarf evergreens are smothered in late spring with a profusion of bright or pastel flowers. A single plant, such as the red 'Hino-Crimson,' the softer-hued 'Pink Pearl,' or the white 'Snow,' makes a spectacular focal point in a foliage grouping of ground-hugging cotoneasters and low *Euonymus fortunei* 'Silver Queen,' with hostas and *Ajuga reptans* for ground cover.

▲ **White and gold** The variegated evergreen shrub *Euonymus fortunei radicans* creates pools of light. Its companion here is the trout lily *(Erythronium revolutum* 'White Beauty'), with its large mottled leaves and white, yellow-centered flowers.

▼ **White and red** North-facing sites can be problematic, but the climbing *Hydrangea petiolaris* thrives in such settings, bearing large clusters of greenish-white flowers in summer. The scarlet-flowered perennial *Tropaeolum speciosum* needs similar conditions.

▲ **Height of summer** Yellow potentilla glows against *Lonicera nitida* 'Baggesen's Gold' and lavender-blue *Iris pallida*.

◀ **Shrubby cinquefoils** The dainty *Potentilla fruticosa* is in flower for most of the summer. Here, it fronts a white-and-blue composition that includes tall, creamy white *Aruncus dioicus* and steel-blue *Eryngium alpinum*. A flat-topped spirea adds a touch of vibrant russet-red.

▼ **Depths of winter** *Fagus sylvatica* 'Purpurea Pendula,' a golden juniper, and an evergreen hebe stand silvered by frost.

▲ **Hanging basket** The frost-tender *Fuchsia* 'Marinka,' with its deep red flowers, is ideal for trailing over baskets in the company of blue lobelias.

◀ **Hardy in zone 7** The 1 ft (30 cm) tall, red-and-mauve *Fuchsia* 'Tom Thumb' is daringly combined with orange-red nasturtiums. Silver-gray *Santolina chamaecyparissus* has a calming effect.

◀ **Hardy fuchsia** In the mild climates of the South and the Pacific Coast, *Fuchsia magellanica* is a superb shrub for garden color. Here the cultivar 'Winston Churchill' furnishes a splendid backdrop for the dahlia 'Tequila Sunrise.'

SMALL SHRUBS

Shrubs are the key to a garden that looks good year-round; even the smallest area will welcome a selection of these hardworking plants.

Although flowering perennials and annuals are important for color and interest in the growing season — from late spring until the first fall frosts — shrubs, whether evergreen or deciduous, are on show 12 months a year. Being permanent, they are particularly valuable from midfall to midspring, when they are the principal source of color and texture. But whatever the season, shrubs give added depth and shape to the garden.

By choosing carefully, you can make the most of the year-round presence of shrubs. The majority are grown for their floral display, and, climate permitting, you can have shrubs in flower year round. However, shrubs have much more to offer: brightly colored berries or bark; unusual spring or fall leaf coloring; fragrant flowers or aromatic leaves; evergreen foliage or, if deciduous, a winter framework of branches that often forms a lacelike tracery.

▲ **Rock roses** This hybrid *Cistus* is a low, spreading shrub that bears a succession of satiny crimson-blotched flowers throughout midsummer.

▼ **Summer shrubs** *Weigela florida* 'Foliis Purpureus,' with its deep pink flowers and purple-flushed leaves, dominates a grouping of potentilla, golden spiraea, and lavender.

▲ **Cinquefoil** Indispensable in the garden, the shrubby cinquefoils *(Potentilla fruticosa)* are ultrahardy (to zone 3) and tolerant of all types of soil. The dwarf cultivar 'Red Ace' grows best in light shade. It bears bright orange-red flowers from late spring into fall.

▼ **Wild lilac** Handsome foliage (evergreen in many species) and a springtime show of lilaclike blossoms have made our native ceanothuses a favorite shrub of the Southwest. These plants' tolerance for drought makes them a practical choice, too.

▲ **Winter colors** Dogwoods are most dramatic in winter, when their bare but colored branches bring life to a garden. Red-stemmed *Cornus alba* 'Sibirica' and yellow-stemmed *C. stolonifera* 'Flaviramea' must be pruned hard in spring to encourage vivid new growth. Both have insignificant white flowers and dark green leaves *(below)*.

Shrubs for small gardens

Where space is at a premium, it is best to choose shrubs that have several interesting features. The bright yellow springtime flowers of *Mahonia aquifolium,* for example, are followed by blue-black berries in summer. These, combined with its glossy evergreen leaves and architectural shape, make the shrub a focal point in the garden all year.

Height and growth rate

The smaller the garden, the more important the choice of shrubs becomes. Always find out the potential height of a shrub *before* buying it. Some shrubs, such as American holly *(Ilex opaca),* eventually become large trees if left to their own devices. However, with regular pruning their size may be contained for many years.

How quickly a shrub grows is as important as its ultimate height, so consider both factors together. Forsythias and camellias, for example, have much the same potential height (8 ft/2.4 m), but the former may take 4 or 5 years to reach it, the latter 15 or even 20 years. Many shrubs lose their appeal with age and are therefore best discarded.

Very often — particularly if the garden is relatively new — choosing shrubs becomes a balancing act: quick growth gives an established look to an otherwise bare plot of earth, but a shrub that outgrows its fair share of space within 4 or 5 years is a bad long-term choice.

Growing conditions — the amount of nutrients and moisture in the soil, sunlight, wind exposure, and surrounding space available — affect the height and growth rate of a shrub. The most extreme example is the art of bonsai, in which potentially huge trees are miniaturized by container growing, rigorous pruning, and strict feeding regimes.

While control on such a scale is not possible with garden shrubs, it is generally true that a shrub whose roots are confined grows more slowly than one with room to spread its roots. The same is true of shrubs growing in soil lacking in nutrients, but starving a shrub to keep it small will quickly result in a weak plant vulnerable to pests and diseases.

As a guideline for gardens where space is limited, even the

largest "backbone" shrubs should have a maximum height, whether potential or prunable, of 8 ft (2.4 m). A shrub of this height creates screening at and slightly above eye level, and provides a pleasant sense of enclosure without excluding too much light or creating a feeling of claustrophobia.

Certain shrubs, such as rue, fuchsia, and Russian sage *(Perovskia atriplicifolia),* die back to ground level in northern winters, like herbaceous perennials, or are so straggly at the end of winter that they need to be cut back severely to encourage attractive new growth. While these plants are valuable during the summer months, don't rely on them for a "shrubby" year-round presence in the garden.

Shape and spread

The spread of a shrub is as important as its height, especially in a very small garden. Choose shrubs that have a diameter of less than 8 ft (2.4 m), and even smaller in tiny gardens. A wide-spreading shrub can smother weaker nearby plants with its rampant growth. Some shrubs, such as fatsia, however, may have wide-spreading top growth that springs from sparse, narrow, and largely upright stems, so shade-loving ground-cover plants can flourish under its canopy. Other shrubs, such as cinquefoil *(Potentilla),* appear thick and dense at ground level, with no room for underplanting.

If space is short, it is tempting to choose only rigidly upright shrubs. However, a balanced contrast of shapes — such as an upright rosemary grown near a dome-shaped senecio and low mounds of lavender cotton, is considerably more effective.

Choosing flowering shrubs

Although catalogs tend to illustrate shrubs in flower, remember that shrubs spend more of the year displaying berries and foliage. However, if blossoms are what you want, some, such as lavender, are long-lasting and will continue for weeks. Others, such as rock rose *(Cistus),* have flowers that are individually short-lived, but are produced for many weeks.

Also consider whether the leaves are evergreen or deciduous — a general rule of thumb is to have evergreen plants compose

▲ **Fire thorn** *Pyracantha coccinea* is ideal for small gardens as it takes up little space and responds well to pruning. The creamy white flowers in summer and red, orange, or yellow berries in fall are annual highlights.

▶**Seaside shrubs** The New Zealand hebes won't overwinter reliably north of zone 8, but are tolerant of salt-laden sea sprays. With their clusters of white to pink flowers, they are summertime stars in California and the coastal Southeast.

▼ **Scarlet and white** The acid-loving evergreen *Pieris formosa* creates its own color combinations in late spring. The young scarlet leaves are enhanced by older, glossy-green foliage and white bell-shaped flowers.

50 percent of the garden, to see it through fall, winter, and early spring. (An all-evergreen garden can be too somber; one devoid of evergreens is bare for much of the year.)

If the garden has enough color and interest from annuals and perennials in summer, choose shrubs that come into their own when the summer display is over. For example, the Japanese quince *(Chaenomeles speciosa)* bears white, pink, or red spring flowers; yellow fruits in fall; and an irregular exotic-looking growth habit, seen at its best in the winter months. The colorful stems of the red-barked dogwood *(Cornus alba* 'Sibirica') also provide winter interest when leafless.

Winter flowers (where they thrive) are often more striking than those of summer species,

▶ **Blue accent** Outstanding among ornamental grasses, arching clumps of blue-green *Festuca ovina* 'Glauca' add charm to any garden. Blue bell-shaped flowers emphasize the color scheme.

▼ **Silver foliage** The centerpiece in this formal bed is a standard-trained *Artemisia arborescens.* It rises nobly from a bed of scarlet petunias rimmed with silvered tufts of *Senecio cineraria.*

simply because of their rarity. One camellia bush in flower is worth dozens of bedding plants, especially if it is visible from the living room.

Colored foliage

Both evergreen and deciduous shrubs have leaves in a variety of colors, ranging from silvery white and gray (lavender cotton, or *Santolina*) to creamy yellow and deep gold *(Viburnum opulus* 'Aureum'), and even red-purple *(Berberis thunbergii* 'Atropurpurea').

Gray and silver plants are both attractive and widely available. There is a huge range of gray-leaved shrubs, including artemisias, lavenders, santolinas, senecios, helichrysums, rock roses, hebes, potentillas, and willows. There are also gray-leaved cultivars of familiar plants such as gray-leaved heather *(Calluna vulgaris* 'Silver Queen') and gray-leaved *Rosa glauca*.

Of the trees, weeping silver pear *(Pyrus salicifolia* 'Pendula') is perhaps the best choice for small gardens. For large gardens there are eucalyptuses, willows, especially *Salix alba argentea* (also listed as 'Sericea'), and several cultivars of *Populus alba*.

Popular perennials include lamb's ears *(Stachys byzantina), Achillea* 'Moonshine,' pearly everlastings, *Festuca ovina* 'Glauca,' and *Hosta sieboldiana*. Sea hollies *(Eryngium),* anthemis, globe thistle, *Veronica incana,* cardoon, and globe artichoke are other options.

Gray-leaved biennials and

▲ **Bloodleaf** The aptly named *Iresine herbstii* is a shrubby perennial that is evergreen in frost-free areas. Its blood-red, prominently veined leaves on bright red stems benefit from the calming influence of the trailing silver-gray stems of helichrysum.

▶ **Silver carpet** As ground cover, the silver-leaved *Tanacetum haradjanii* offers dramatic contrast to darker foliage plants, such as the ornamental woolly-leaved sage *(Salvia argentea)*.

annuals include mulleins *(Verbascum),* giant thistles *(Onopordum),* horned poppies, and silver-leaved cineraria *(Senecio cineraria).* There are gray-leaved rock garden pinks, saxifrages, sedums, androsaces, antennarias, and sempervivums. Dwarf forms of achillea, artemisia, chrysanthemum, and helichrysum provide delicate gray foliage at the front of borders.

Using gray-leaved plants

Gray-leaved foliage varies widely in size, shape, and texture. There are smooth and even fleshy gray-leaved plants — for example, succulent houseleeks and stonecrops. Some gray-leaved plants look like lace, such as *Tanacetum densum* 'Amani'; others have enormous leaves, such as giant thistles and mulleins.

Gray-leaved plants are excellent for soothing and cooling down hot colors — fiery oranges, pinks, reds, and purples. Gray foliage is especially good with late-summer and fall blooms such as dahlias, cosmos, zinnias, and hollyhocks. It is equally effective in cooling down the hot foliage colors of purple *Cotinus coggygria,* purple barberry, and staghorn sumac, which turns a fiery red in the fall.

Most plants with pale gray,

▲ **Foliage displays** Variegated *Euonymus fortunei,* glossy green mahonia, silvery senecio, and purple berberis provide year-round color.

▼ **Garland flower** The prostrate *Daphne cneorum,* sweet-scented and rose-pink, flowers with the brooms.

white, or silver leaves automatically attract the eye. (The darker blue-leaved rue and *Hosta sieboldiana* are less prominent.) As automatic focal points, such plants need very careful siting. Sprinkling them around a garden often results in a discordant, disjointed effect. Gray-leaved plants show up best against a dark background, such as a conifer hedge or a brick wall.

In gray and silver beds, or gray areas in a mixed bed, try to include several different plants, for added variety. A bed composed entirely of silvery filigree foliage is likely to appear flat, especially on overcast days. But a bed or border with round, filigree, and sword-shaped foliage in a range of silvers, grays, whites, and blues, and in a variety of textures and plant heights, is inevitably rich in both depth and detail.

Gray-leaved plants need light soil that is not too fertile, otherwise the leaves grow lush and green. They also need direct sunlight. Their silver, gray, white, or blue color is a protective measure to reduce transpiration in wind and hot summer sun, while shade has the opposite effect, encouraging more lush green growth. Gray plants also grow lanky in shade, in their search for light.

CLIMBING COMPANY

Even in a limited space, climbers — woody, herbaceous, perennial, or annual — can form stunning associations with other climbers and shrubs of different habits.

Climbers add an extra dimension to a garden and are very useful in smaller gardens, where space is limited. They can partner one another, create a beautiful covering for undistinguished or unsightly walls and fences, enhance pergolas and arches, or climb poles in a mixed border.

True climbers, mainly woody types but also some herbaceous species, are characterized by weak, lax stems that need support to keep them upright. Some climbers, such as ivies and ornamental vines, are self-clinging; others, like clematises and sweet peas, are equipped with tendrils that attach themselves to any available support. Yet others, such as climbing and rambling roses and winter jasmine, cannot support themselves and therefore must be tied into place.

Climbing plants can play many roles in the garden. In addition to hiding eyesores and complementing existing features, they can add a touch of beauty to old fruit trees — for example, allow clematis and roses to scramble through their branches. They can also bring new life to daunting north-facing sites. Ivies, climbing hydrangeas, the purple-flowered *Akebia quinata,* and all *Parthenocissus* species flourish in such shady spots.

Climbers grow at different rates and should be in proportion to their supports. Wisteria easily reaches a spread of 50 ft (15 m) when well established, and the twice-yearly pruning required to encourage the production of flowering shoots can be a daunting task. Where wall space is limited, *Jasminum nudiflorum* or sweet-scented honeysuckle is much easier to control.

The hardy silver-lace vine *(Polygonum aubertii)* is very vig-

▶ **Pure passion** The summer-blooming passionflower *(Passiflora caerulea)* climbs rapidly in light, evenly moist soils in sheltered spots (in zone 8 and south). It bears large white flowers with purple centers. Evergreen, purple-flowered *Daphne odora* 'Aureo-marginata'and *Potentilla* 'Elizabeth' with yellow blooms provide color at the base of the passionflower.

55

▲ **Exuberant scrambler** Left to its own devices, clematis will take support where it finds it, clambering up trees, twining around shrubs, or scrambling among companions in mixed borders. The vivid color of this large-flowered hybrid is softened by silver-gray artemisias.

◀ **Wall companions** Given a large expanse of shady wall, the honeysuckle *Lonicera* x *tellmanniana* will quickly climb to a height of 15 ft (4.5 m) or more. Its spectacular clusters of glowing copper-yellow flowers in midsummer blend well with *Clematis* 'Mrs. Cholmondeley,' whose soft blue flowers continue well into fall — when the leaves of the ornamental grape, *Vitis coignetiae*, begin to turn vivid crimson.

▶ **Shades of pink** The exotic-looking *Actinidia kolomikta* is a vigorous climbing vine, with magnificent tricolored leaves of dark green, pink, and white. It is accompanied by a tall escallonia, whose drooping racemes of deep pink tubular flowers perfectly match the vine's unusual leaf colors.

orous. It is a popular choice because of its capacity to smother everything in its path with clouds of greenish-white flowers. Plant it with discretion, choosing a place where it can tumble at will without interfering with other plants in your garden.

Clematis, the queen of climbers, likes company. The large-flowered hybrids that adorn pillars, pergolas, and walls combine well with climbing roses and green ivies, while the smaller-flowered clematis species ramble naturally among shrubs and trees. The nodding purple bells of *Clematis viticella* look delightful with the flat heads of white or pink lace-cap hydrangeas or *Viburnum plicatum*. The scrambling *C. tangutica*, with its wonderful combination of yellow lantern flowers and silky seed heads, looks even better when paired with the tubular orange blooms of climbing Chilean glory flower *(Eccremocarpus scaber).*

Ivies are sympathetic partners. Few plants can rival the variegated *Hedera helix* 'Goldheart' ('Jubilee') for brightening up a wall. It has small green leaves splashed with a yellow that never fades and gleams in the shade. This ivy is perfect for clothing a garden wall when mixed with *Tropaeolum speciosum* for bright scarlet summer color. *Hedera colchica* 'Dentata Variegata,' another type of variegated ivy, is notably vigorous, easily covering a wall 20-30 ft (6-9 m) high and bearing the largest leaves of all ivies, edged with broad creamy yellow borders.

Herbaceous climbers
Several annuals, in addition to sweet peas, climb rapidly and are ideal for summer screens. These plants will grow on their own along wire-mesh or pillar supports, or against ivy-covered garden walls. The cup-and-saucer plant *(Cobaea scandens)* reaches

up to 12 ft (3.6 m) and produces large bell-shaped flowers, which change from green to purple by the end of summer. Morning glory *(Ipomoea tricolor)* grows to 8 ft (2.4 m) in a sunny spot and bears blue trumpet flowers, which open every morning.

Perennial climbers include the everlasting pea *(Lathyrus latifolius)*, which grows up to 10 ft (3 m) tall and bears rose-purple flowers that mix well with yellow daylilies and blue *Salvia* × *superba*. The golden hop *(Humulus lupulus* 'Aureus') can reach 20 ft (6 m) in a single season and is ideal for training up pergolas together with large-flowered clematis hybrids.

▼ **Clematis clones** Large-flowered clematis hybrids, such as the petunia-red 'Ernest Markham' and the violet 'Mrs. N. Thompson,' make a glorious show grouped with the dainty yellow flower lanterns and silvery seed heads of *Clematis tangutica.*

◄ **Arched profusion** Pink and scarlet sweet peas *(Lathyrus odoratus)* scramble through ripening squashes trained up a metal pergola. Massive sunflowers nod from above, as if recognizing other members of the daisy family — the golden rudbeckias that line the path.

► **Tree climber** The rampant *Clematis montana* is festooned in late spring with a mass of starry white flowers. It grows happily on a north-facing wall and will clamber through tall trees. Here, its flowers mingle with the yellow drapes of *Laburnum* x *watereri.*

▼ **Fall glory** The self-clinging Boston ivy *(Parthenocissus tricuspidata)* is a familiar sight on house walls. It is a source of delight when the leaves turn crimson and scarlet before falling in fall. The cream-edged leaves of its evergreen partner, the Canary Island ivy *(Hedera canariensis* 'Variegata'), provide a good contrast.

▲ **Accommodating ivy** The common ivy *(Hedera helix)* grows as ground cover or wall covering in the most inhospitable places. Golden cultivars like 'Buttercup' add splashes of light to dull sites and provide excellent support for clematises, such as *Clematis montana* 'Rubens.'

▶ **Pillar climbers** Choose climbers of moderate vigor for low pergolas and pillars; otherwise the floral display will be above eye level. Clematis and honeysuckle make good partners and can be kept within bounds with annual pruning.

▼ **'Nelly Moser'** One of the most popular clematises, 'Nelly Moser' flowers twice — in early and late summer. A young specimen combines well with nicotianas.

▶ **Sweet welcome** Roses and clematises make classic partnerships. Here, a 'New Dawn' rose climbs up to meet blue *Clematis* x *jackmanii* 'Superba' to create a delightful summer framework.

◀ **Sweet peas** The ever-popular sweet peas *(Lathyrus odoratus)* flower from early summer to early fall on plants that may climb as high as 10 ft (3 m). Sweet peas can be trained up a fence or trellis, but they look more appealing at the rear of borders, where their flowers create a colorful tapestry for other plants. Available in mixed and single colors, sweet peas provide an unending supply of cut flowers if regularly deadheaded.

This multicolored group is appropriately fronted by pastel shades — pale lemon lady's mantle *(Alchemilla mollis)* and dwarf blue-and-white *Convolvulus tricolor.*

▼ **Morning glory** The common morning glory *(Ipomoea purpurea)* is a half-hardy annual, but in its brief growing season it will climb to a height of 10 ft (3 m) if sited against a sunny fence. Here, its mass of purple trumpet flowers is exquisitely partnered by another annual climber, the yellow-flowered canary creeper *(Tropaeolum peregrinum),* a relative of the common nasturtium. The creeper reaches much the same height as the morning glory and provides brilliant contrasts in flower shape and color.

◀ **Vermilion nasturtium** A relative of the familiar annual, the vermilion nasturtium *(Tropaeolum speciosum)* is a hardy perennial climber. It thrives in acid soil, especially when its roots are in shade and its flowers in sun. Good companions include ivies, spring-flowering *Bergenia* 'Silberlicht,' and *Gentiana asclepiadea,* which bears deep blue flowers in summer.

ROSES LIKE COMPANY

**Although frequently condemned to solitary confinement,
grown on their own and surrounded by bare earth,
roses look attractive in mixed beds, against a background
of complementary flowers and foliage.**

There are roses for every garden and almost any garden position. Some, like the old-fashioned shrub roses, have one short though exquisitely fragrant flowering season in early summer, which is followed by brightly colored hips in fall. Others, modern bush roses and climbers for example, are in bloom almost continuously from early summer until the fall frosts.

The rose is widely acclaimed as the "queen of flowers." Yet it is worth taking time to consider where to place this beauty in the garden. Some roses are so splendid in bloom and in form that they deserve to be grown as specimen shrubs. Others, like bush roses, look stunning partnered by their own kind. Shrub roses are set off to perfection in a mixed border in the company of well-chosen perennials and shrubs.

The growth pattern of roses is as diverse as their form. Some roses hug the ground, rooting and spreading as they grow; others fit neatly into rock garden pockets; still others clamber 30 ft (10 m) or more up tall trees and house walls; and yet others lace their prickly branches so closely together that they form a dense barrier hedge.

Traditional layouts

In formal beds roses are set in a strict pattern. Bush roses (hybrid tea roses and floribundas) grow well under these conditions, as they do not have to compete with other permanent plants for soil moisture and nutrients. Sited in an island bed, they benefit from good light and air circulation and are also much easier to manage in terms of pruning, mulching, and deadheading. In addition, their massed blooming in formal beds has more impact than if they are grown singly.

Hybrid tea roses and floribundas do not mix well, because the cluster-flowered floribundas are more vigorous and spreading. Grow them in separate beds, and for the most pleasing results, stick to types that harmonize both in habit and color.

One drawback with rose beds is the amount of bare soil that is visible. Underplant with low-growing bedding plants to overcome this problem — try alyssum or lobelias, compact ageratums, dwarf marigolds, and impatiens. Traditional rose beds are frequently edged with low, primly pruned hedges of box or lavender. For winter and early-spring interest, the bare ground can be covered with snowdrops, miniature irises, or crocuses.

Roses in borders

In the past, shrub roses were used in large formal plantings, but they

▶ **Formal rose bed** A color scheme of pink, blue, and green is dominated by the large-flowered hybrid tea rose 'Madame Butterfly.' The shell-pink, yellow-flushed rose is grown in an island bed edged with clipped mounds of blue-gray rue (*Ruta graveolens* 'Jackman's Blue'). Blue bedding pansies (*Viola x wittrockiana*) cover the ground beneath the roses.

With rigorous deadheading, the roses will provide color from early spring through summer and into fall.

▲ **'Golden Scepter'** This large-flowered bush rose can be rather gawky in appearance, as its spindly stems are only sparsely clothed with foliage. It is best planted in a shrub border where low-growing foliage plants can conceal its base. Here, it rises like a bright yellow beacon above clumps of purple-leaved sage (*Salvia officinalis* 'Purpurascens').

▲ **'Constance Spry'** The large, fully double flowers of this vigorous shrub rose are clear pink and heavily scented. Borne in early summer to midsummer, they associate well with hardy geraniums such as *Geranium pratense* 'Johnson's Blue,' valued for its dark green, deeply cut leaves and clear blue flowers.

◄ **'Queen Elizabeth'** This well-known floribunda rose forms a tall, stiff bush, 6 ft (1.8 m) or more in height. It bears most of its sweet-scented flowers at the crown. Their deep pink color is displayed to perfection against a backdrop of dark conifers. The leggy stems can be shrouded by a suitable foreground — here, blue-flowered rosemary (*Rosmarinus officinalis*), 3 ft (90 cm) high, is joined by clumps of lower-growing lavender (*Lavandula angustifolia* 'Hidcote').

can look equally good incorporated in small shrub or mixed borders. They have many advantages over bedding roses — they need only light pruning, for instance, and are comparable to the best flowering shrubs. As with other shrubs, modern and old-fashioned shrub roses are most striking in groups of three or more.

In mixed borders intermingle shrub roses with perennials that have striking foliage as well as attractive flowers. Lady's mantle, for example, is excellent for camouflaging the unsightly stems of some shrub roses. Silvery plants and evergreens look particularly attractive with roses, either as an

edging at the front of the border or interplanted. Both provide interest over a long period — silver foliage during summer and evergreens year-round.

Some wonderful effects can be achieved with a background planting of delphiniums. Their elegant blue spires look very effective with pink, white, and red shrub roses. For a more subtle effect, try the plume poppy *(Macleaya cordata)*, with its delicate pink-buff flowers and green-silver leaves. This plant produces a subtle effect when grown behind a creamy orange rose such as 'Buff Beauty,' and this long-lasting color combination delights the eye

throughout the summer months.

Old-fashioned roses often flower only once a year, usually in early summer to midsummer. For the most spectacular effect, select partners that bloom at the same time as the roses but keep their flowers longer, thus diverting attention from the roses' fading beauty.

For old-style roses with attractive foliage and colorful hips, consider *Rosa moyesii, R. glauca,* and *R. xanthina* 'Canary Bird.' Rugosa hybrid roses do double duty as hedging plants and are real gems in the shrub border. Generally around 5 ft (1.5 m) high, they are outstanding for their rich green, heavily veined foliage and their heady fragrance. The pink 'Fru Dagmar Hastrup' and the crimson 'Scabrosa' bear large decorative hips with the last of the flower crop. 'Roseraie de l'Hay,' considered the finest rugosa rose, deserves a place in any shrub border.

Old-fashioned rose blooms are often much flatter and rounder than the newer bush roses (hybrid teas and floribundas). This flower form — and the soft colors associated with old roses — can be pleasantly enhanced by a closely planted mixture of contrasting flower shapes. You can try columbines in shades of red, blue, pink, and purple; the tall spikes of delphiniums or foxgloves; blue and white *Campanula persicifolia;* and later in the year, delicate pink or white Japanese anemones.

To complement the pretty flower form of old shrub roses, try planting double peonies, cranesbills such as *Geranium pratense* 'Johnson's Blue,' and scented pinks, which will all add to the cottage-garden effect.

Effective long-flowering shrubs to combine with old-style roses include lavender and *Potentilla fruticosa*, or any of the hardier rock roses *(Cistus* species).

Gray- and silver-leaved plants such as artemisia, lavender cotton *(Santolina chamaecyparissus)*, and *Stachys byzantina* form

◀ **Old-fashioned roses** The long, arching stems of the gallica rose 'Complicata' are laden with large, bright pink flowers in early summer. The color blends effectively with the tubular blooms of another old-fashioned charmer, tall-growing foxgloves.

▼ **Red and white companions** The elegant species rose *Rosa moyesii,* up to 10 ft (3 m) tall, is a favorite specimen shrub. In early summer its blood-red flowers glow against creamy white spikes of the evergreen Portugal laurel *(Prunus lusitanica).* At ground level, fans of *Cotoneaster horizontalis* display tiny leaves and small pink flowers.

▲ **First rose of summer** The arching and bristly stems of *Rosa* 'Cantabrigiensis' form the centerpiece in this early-summer scene. The shrub is endowed with dainty fernlike foliage and blooms of the softest yellow. Here, it towers above deep blue belladonna delphiniums and sprawling clumps of white and pale purple dame's rocket *(Hesperis matronalis).*

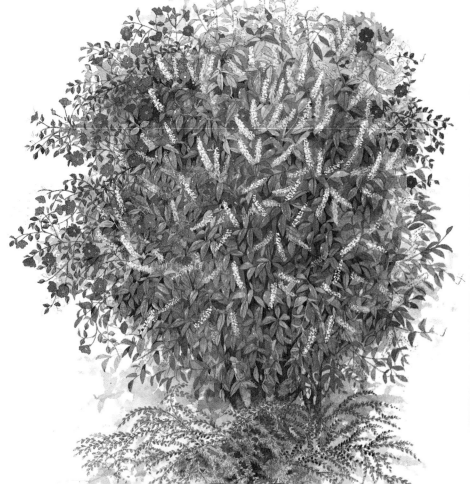

▼ **Hybrid musk roses** Popular for their heady fragrance and long flowering season, musk roses like 'Penelope' are of vigorous arching habit. The enormous flower trusses are deep pink in the bud, open to pale pink, and fade to creamy white, forming an excellent backdrop for the steel-blue flower heads of the globe thistle *(Echinops ritro)*.

At the foot of the group, the bright magenta blooms and silvery foliage of campion *(Lychnis coronaria)* complete the color composition.

▲ **Dainty bloomer** Resembling apple blossom, 'Ballerina' has large sprays of pale pink, white-eyed flowers in summer and fall. Rarely exceeding 4 ft (1.2 m) in height and spread, this dainty shrub is at home in a mixed border. Here, its delicate colors are complemented by the gray-green foliage and lavender-blue flowers of catmint *(Nepeta x faassenii)*.

▼ **Mixing old and new** The splendid rugosa rose 'Roseraie de l'Hay' flowers almost continuously from early summer to fall. Its tall branches set with crimson-purple flowers make a rich background for the hybrid musk rose 'Erfurt.' This, too, is deliciously scented, carmine-red, and creamy-eyed. Double-flowered peonies add to a symphony of red and pink, which includes the gallica rose 'Complicata' on the left.

◀ **Bourbon roses** Typified by their large bowl-shaped blooms and intense fragrance, bourbon roses flower intermittently from early summer until the fall frosts. 'Mme. Isaac Pereire' bears distinctive deep pink, quartered flowers. This large shrub is ideal for background planting.

Clumps of *Geranium endressii* flower simultaneously with the roses and make worthy companions with their deeply divided leaves and clear pink blooms.

▶ **Pillar rose** Left to its own devices and tied loosely to a tall, strong stake, the hybrid musk rose 'Buff Beauty' will arch its 6 ft (1.8 m) tall branches like a fountain. The sweetly scented flowers are creamy yellow, darkening to apricot, and are carried in great profusion in early summer and midsummer, with a second display in early fall.

Such soft colors demand companions that will not detract from the shrub's beauty in bloom. Here, it rises in summer from a sea of blue-flowered catmint (*Nepeta* x *faassenii*) pierced with black-eyed white poppies (*Papaver orientale* 'Perry's White') and the soft golden and red-brown flags of a bearded iris.

▲ **Power in numbers** Miniature roses are most effective when planted in groups. Together, the mauve blossoms of 'Sweet Chariot,' the golden flowers of 'Orange Honey,' and the striped 'Two-Timer' achieve a border of charming informality.

▲ **Traditional partnership**
A tumbling profusion of climbing and rambling roses forms the perfect background for tall perennials such as delphiniums. Vigorous rambling roses such as 'Wedding Day,' seen here trailing over a wall, are ideal for growing up trees. The large clusters of lemon-white flowers are sweetly scented.

◀ **Old favorites** The vigorous 'Albertine' is one of the most popular of the rambling roses. It is clothed with a mass of richly scented, double coppery pink flowers in early summer. Afterward, the display here is continued for several more weeks as the rugosa rose 'Scabrosa' unfolds its large, single crimson-purple flowers.
    The roses here are excellent for clothing fences and walls — and the rugosas are good hedging, too. Their bases are hidden by a tumbling planting of red valerians (*Centranthus ruber*) and white feverfews (*Tanacetum parthenium*).

◄ Yellow-and-blue symphony
The hybrid species rose 'Harison's Yellow,' an easygoing shrub up to 6 ft (1.8 m) tall, is resplendent in early summer with large semidouble flowers of clear yellow. As the rose begins to fade, its companion, the ornamental potato vine *(Solanum crispum),* comes into bloom, producing large clusters of yellow-eyed purple-blue flowers well into late summer and fall.

▼ Golden showers Subtle color combinations can be as effective as strong contrasts. This partnership between yellow climbing roses and the strong-growing honeysuckle *(Lonicera x tellmanniana),* with its coppery yellow flowers, is soothing to the eye and particularly restful on hot summer days. The group displays subtle differences in leaf texture and flower color and density. Climbing yellow roses for similar matches include 'Dreaming Spires,' 'Golden Showers,' 'Mermaid,' and 'Schoolgirl.'

a soft carpet around the base of thorny stems and complement the delicate shades of old-fashioned roses.

Other good foliage partners include the evergreen purple-leaved sage *(Salvia officinalis* 'Purpurascens'), soft-textured *Alchemilla mollis*, bold hostas, and sprawling grayish-green catmint *(Nepeta × faassenii).*

For a striking contrast to the mounded form of many shrub roses, use the distinctive swordlike foliage of irises or the smaller *Sisyrinchium striatum*, whose creamy flowers complement yellow or white roses.

Standards and miniatures
Standard roses are hybrid teas or floribundas grafted onto tall, bare stems of some sturdy rootstock rose. Weeping standards are rambling roses budded onto a standard stem. All standards are used mostly as accent plants to give

height to beds and freestanding borders of bush roses, annuals, and low-growing perennials. They can also be grown on their own as specimen plants.

Standard roses look particularly spectacular in beds flanking a driveway or broad path, with the ground beneath occupied by annuals, compact perennials, silver-leaved foliage plants, or dwarf forms of lavender.

Miniature roses, dainty replicas of their hybrid tea and floribunda relations, are at the other end of the scale. Ranging in height from 3-18 in (7.5-45 cm), they come in all the usual rose shades and as bicoloreds, too. Although they can be used to edge beds and borders, their charm is more obvious if they are sited at eye level — in raised beds, rock gardens, and window boxes. Set them out in groups for greater impact, as the effect of a single plant is often lost.

Rose hedges
Many roses are particularly suitable for hedging and barriers, the best being the shrubby types, which need little if any pruning and whose strong stems can be allowed to interlace. Like other deciduous hedging plants, roses lose their leaves in winter but still form effective wind screens, and most of them flower throughout the summer months.

For barrier hedges, few can rival the rugosa hybrid roses when given some support. Their prickly stems will keep all intruders at a distance. Some, such as 'Blanc Double de Coubert' and 'Roseraie de l'Hay,' form dense thickets up to 8 ft (2.4 m) high.

For a medium-size hedge, 4-6 ft

▼ **Rose garden** There are no limits to the true rosarian's passion for roses. Climbers, ramblers, shrubs, and bushes display variations in the shape, color, and texture of the incomparable rose.

(1.2-1.8 m) high, choose another fragrant musk rose, the silver-pink 'Felicia,' or rugosa hybrid roses such as 'Rubra,' the white single 'Alba,' or the semidouble 'Schneezwerg.'

Interior or edging hedges, dividing one part of the garden from another, should be kept comparatively low. Use small repeat-flowering shrub roses, such as the vigorous pink 'Bonica 82' and the red, white-eyed 'Fiona,' which do not grow much above 3 ft (90 cm). Alternative choices include the pale pink centifolia 'Rose de Meaux' and the rose-pink gallica rose 'Empress Josephine,' although these roses flower only once in the season.

Hybrid teas and floribundas, with their erect growth, are not reliably wind resistant on exposed sites, and they need severe annual pruning if they are to flower abundantly. The popular floribunda 'Queen Elizabeth' is sometimes used as a hedge. It is strong and vigorous, but when left unpruned, it tends to grow leggy and flower less freely.

Climbing roses

You can train climbing roses on house walls and fences, pergolas, pillars and arches, rustic screens, and tall trees. By the nature of their growth, they need strong

▲ **Prostrate roses** The sprawling habit of some modern shrub roses makes them ideal for covering banks. Here, the 3 ft (90 cm) high 'Raubritter' is used in a formal island bed, where interplanting would break up the uniform scheme.

▼ **Weeping standards** Grafted onto bare stems, 5-6 ft (1.5-1.8 m) tall, of a sturdy rootstock rose and trained over an umbrella-shaped wire frame, rambler roses trail elegantly to the ground. A rose standard makes a stunning focal point.

and sturdy support. In addition, their shoots may need to be tied regularly. Deadhead them frequently to keep them looking their best.

Climbers' performance (their vigor, hardiness, eventual height, and flowering display) depends largely on their complex origins. Before ordering a climber for a particular situation, check catalogs from various reputable rose growers.

Repeat-flowering "sports" climbers (those that developed as spontaneous mutations of one branch of a hybrid tea rose) are very vigorous climbers and are particularly suitable for house walls. When well established, they average 15 ft (4.5 m) in height and are often more spectacular in bloom than their bushy relatives,

▶ **Rose-clad arch** Richly scented repeat-flowering climbers of moderate vigor are ideal for romantic arbors, pillars, and arches.

▼ **Miniature climber** Deprived of upright support, the climbing miniature rose 'Nozomi' forms a spreading ground-cover shrub, densely set with clusters of pearly pink blooms.

especially the crimson 'Climbing Étoile de Hollande' and the soft pink 'Climbing Cécile Brünner.'

Most modern repeat-flowering climbers average about 10 ft (3 m) in height and bear more or less continuous clusters of semi-double or fully double blossoms. They are particularly ideal for growing up walls, pillars, and rustic screens. Some cultivars, such as 'Danse du Feu,' 'Golden Showers,' 'Mermaid,' and 'New Dawn,' are suitable for northern-exposure sites.

Rambling roses are of exceptional vigor and reach their full potential only where they can be allowed to clamber unchecked up tall trees and similar structures. Most spectacular is 'Kiftsgate,' whose 30 ft (9 m) long stems are smothered in early summer with creamy white scented flowers. 'Bobbie James' is similar, but has larger blooms, while the apple-scented 'François Juranville' is a glowing pink color. More moderate types, such as the popular 'Albertine' and 'Dorothy Perkins,' will ramble happily over fences and hedges.

Rambler roses flower only once, usually in early summer.

Prune them immediately after flowering — cut back the old-flowered shoots and tie in young replacement shoots.

Combining climbing roses and clematises is a traditional way of having double color on a wall. Honeysuckles can also intermingle with large climbing roses or ramblers for rich scents.

Ground-cover roses

Most so-called ground-cover roses are actually wide-spreading shrub roses whose lower branches hug the ground and smother weeds. They look pretty tumbling over low retaining walls or covering tree stumps.

The rambling *Rosa wichuraiana* is naturally prostrate and will spread widely if allowed to trail along the ground; so, too, will the thorny, white-flowered 'Paulii.' Both are suitable for semiwild gardens or for covering large banks. A more refined look is furnished by two hybrid rugosas: 'Lady Duncan' (bright pink with a yellow center) and 'Max Graf' (clear pink blossoms with a white eye). Both of these grow to a height of just 2 ft (60 cm) but spread their canes

▲**Container roses** Miniature bush roses are ideal for pots, window boxes, and other container gardens. They bloom almost continuously in the summer if regularly deadheaded and fed.

over an area several times that in width. Both display handsome glossy foliage and bloom once a season.

Specimen roses

Old garden roses are perfect for use as specimen plants, as are weeping standards trained on metal frames. However, there are no hard-and-fast rules for which species to choose, although one that flowers prolifically over a long period will be more rewarding. One rose lover will enthuse over the golden and copper-red *Rosa foetida bicolor*, another will swear by *R. moyesii*, whose glistening scarlet blooms are followed with clusters of red bottle-shaped hips. No flower arranger would give up the purple-gray foliage of *R. glauca* (formerly known as *R. rubrifolia*). The rippling sprays of ferny leaves and golden flowers on 'Canary Bird' are also delightful.

Roses in containers

Even a small garden or courtyard can have a display of roses. Several dwarf floribundas and miniature roses are compact enough to grow in troughs, window boxes, and other planters. They do, however, require sun or dappled light — no rose will thrive in dense shade. As with other container plants, they need frequent watering, perfect drainage, and feeding with a commercial liquid rose fertilizer at least once a month during the growing season.

An older group that is well adapted to cultivation in tubs and large planters is the polyantha roses. These compact shrubs are 1-3 ft (30-90 cm) tall and typically are repeat flowering, with small rosette-shaped blossoms in dainty shades of pink, buff, and gold or clear whites and reds.

Partners for rose hips

For many gardeners, the lovely simplicity of species roses is too fleeting, but some of these shrubs come to the fore again in fall, when their fruits appear in contrast to their handsome foliage.

Once the petals have fallen, the hips develop quickly, swelling into globular, bottle, or flask shapes, while their skins ripen to gleaming shades of red, orange, maroon, and purple-black.

These informal shrubs are best in mixed borders with other shrubs and plants chosen to enhance their late-summer beauty.

Rosa rugosa, unlike many species roses, blooms throughout summer. Its last flush of flowers — light pink in 'Fru Dagmar Hastrup,' magenta in 'Scabrosa,' and silky white in 'Alba' — mingles with the fat, round crimson hips. Its deeply veined leaves, turning yellow in fall, look handsome with the foliage of *Cotinus coggygria* 'Royal Purple,' with New York asters planted in front.

The early-summer white or pink flowers of burnet rose *(Rosa spinosissima,* syn. *R. pimpinellifolia)* — a lowish suckering shrub — are followed by purplish-black hips, ¾ in (2 cm) wide, set amid dainty fernlike foliage. White-flowered *Viola cornuta* 'White

Perfection' looks effective weaving among this rose's low-sweeping branches.

Many hip-bearing roses, such as *Rosa glauca* and *R. moyesii,* are bare-stemmed at the base. To hide this feature, plant *Fuchsia magellanica* 'Variegata,' gray artemisias or lavenders, and *Salvia officinalis* 'Purpurea' in front. In addition, *R. moyesii* can be partly hidden by *Aster × frikartii* 'Moench,' whose lavender-blue flowers begin in late summer, or by 3 ft (90 cm) tall, orange-red *Curtonus paniculatus.*

▶ **Fall fruits** Outstanding in flower, foliage, and fruit, deep red *Rosa moyesii* 'Geranium' droops glossy red, flask-shaped hips over a footing of *Vinca major* 'Variegata.'

▶ **Hip flasks** As summer merges into early fall, the splendid *Rosa moyesii* puts on a second spectacular display. The glowing red single flowers with golden centers are replaced by numerous fine flask-shaped fruits that flare into orange-red and droop gracefully from the arching stems.

This vigorous 10 ft (3 m) high shrub rose with its elegant foliage should be planted as a specimen shrub or in a large border, where its stems can mingle with other plants, enhancing them first with flowers and then with hips. A Lawson cypress (*Chamaecyparis lawsoniana* 'Pembury Blue'), for example, creates a misty blue-green foil for the fountain of prickly stems.

The strong vertical emphasis of such a partnership is tempered by the rounded shapes in a foreground planting of *Hydrangea macrophylla* 'Lanarth White.'

▼ **Foliage contrasts** The species rose *Rosa glauca,* formerly known as *R. rubrifolia,* is chiefly grown for its handsome foliage, much prized by flower arrangers. Carried on violet-red stems, the graceful foliage has a bluish-gray sheen that blends attractively with the small red-purple flowers in early summer. In fall the shrub bears smallish red hips.

Such a dainty appearance demands the contrast of stronger foliage plants. Here, bear's breeches (*Acanthus spinosus),* with its deep green leathery and spiny leaves, makes an admirable partner.

▲ **Fall splendor** The rugosa rose 'Fru Dagmar Hastrup' is ideal for small gardens. It is compact, growing at most 5 ft (1.5 m) high and wide; needs little attention; and thrives on sandy soil. The sweetly scented pink flowers open in summer amid wrinkled dark green foliage.

Plump hips appear from late summer onward, before the leaves take on clear yellow fall colors. *Sedum* 'Autumn Joy' makes an attractive companion, with dense flat flower heads maturing through pale pink to deep russet-red.

Border companions

Bulbs, herbaceous perennials, and half-hardy and hardy annuals and biennials display a kaleidoscope of flower colors from spring until late fall. This profusion of color needs careful handling, however, or the effect can be discordant, with clashing colors and badly contrasting flower shapes.

Hardy perennials — which start to grow in spring, flower in summer, and die back in fall before renewing their life cycle — were traditionally displayed on their own, in purely perennial borders. Today, they are more often found in mixed beds and borders, where they may either occupy center stage or play supporting roles among shrubs and foliage plants. They are at their best when framed by foliage to weave a tapestry of complementary colors.

With clever groupings, you can maintain a color scheme for months. For example, plant delphiniums to show off the classic blue spires in early summer, and let their place be taken by clumps of tall bellflowers to continue the blue theme into early fall. Use annuals to fill gaps in borders and add color where early perennials have finished. Sow them directly into the garden or transplant them as seedlings. You can even grow annuals in pots and move them around for instant color wherever it is needed.

Bulbs are invaluable in the garden. With basic gardening care, they can provide a succession of color from late winter through summer and into fall. They take up little room and are effective partners for all other garden plants, from tall trees to ground-hugging ivies. You can find flowering bulbs for every season: daffodils, tulips, and fritillaries bloom in spring; irises and lilies into and through the summer; dahlias and colchicums in fall; and dainty cyclamens and snowdrops in winter.

Summer charm White regal lilies and pink mallow funnels *(Lavatera* 'Silver Cup') add a bright touch to a mixed border.

GARDEN BORDERS

With careful selection, hardy perennials can be grouped to form garden displays offering long-lasting splendor.

Herbaceous borders (also called perennial borders) are an important part of traditional garden design. If skillfully planned, these compositions of perennial flowers furnish a magnificent show all through summer and into fall.

Mixed borders contain shrubs, bulbs, bedding plants, and perennials. A modern development, they arose from a need for a more versatile kind of planting and a desire for long-lasting displays. The bulbs in mixed borders begin flowering earlier in spring than do the traditional border perennials, and so allow the gardener to have color earlier in the season. The addition of annuals ensures continual bloom, even in midsummer, when perennials may temporarily stop flowering. The shrubs, if chosen for colorful

bark and interesting form, will remain attractive in winter. A mixed border, however, cannot equal the visual impact of an old-fashioned herbaceous border at peak bloom.

Mixed or herbaceous borders
Be sure to consider maintenance when choosing between a herbaceous or a mixed border. As a rule, herbaceous borders demand more handwork, such as dead-heading, lifting, and dividing.

The amount of space available should also play a role in your decision. Because herbaceous borders look barren in the winter, they are best adapted to properties with enough room to create distinct areas of seasonal display with separate winter and summer gardens. In small yards, where

▲ **Fall partners** Joe-Pye weed (*Eupatorium purpureum*) is one of the tallest herbaceous plants, reaching a height of 6 ft (1.8 m). Its clusters of purple-pink flowers on purple stems belong in large herbaceous borders. It is also an ideal partner for the blue-flowered *Hydrangea macrophylla*. Both bloom in late summer and fall.

▼ **Pink parfait** The French lavender (*Lavandula stoechas*) makes a pleasant change from the more commonly grown blue English lavender. It flowers earlier and bears purple-pink flower spikes with prominent purple bracts beneath the petals. The pink African daisy (*Osteospermum barberae*) makes a perfect companion.

▶ **Waterside association**
The lush foliage of moisture-loving plants brings a look of well-established maturity to a streamside planting.

In late spring the leafy rosettes of *Primula japonica* support 2 ft (60 cm) tall candelabras of pastel-colored flowers. Alongside these, the magnificent white-edged, boldly ribbed leaves of *Hosta crispula* create an eye-catching centerpoint. Spreading clumps of fernlike astilbes, pale bronze as the leaves unfold, will later replace the faded primula blooms with their fluffy flower spires.

◀ **Shades of gold** The plantain lily *(Hosta fortunei* 'Albo-Picta') is lovely from the moment in spring when its tightly furled leaves open out and become clear yellow with pale green edges. Later, the yellow pales and the green darkens until each leaf is patterned in two shades of green, which take on golden tones with the onset of fall frost. The plant's cool summer elegance blends well with a glorious golden Aurelian lily *(Lilium* x *aurelianense).*

such expansive schemes are impossible, a mixed border is usually more practical.

Formal and informal borders
Formal borders are long, straight-edged rectangles with plants arranged according to color, type, and height — tall plants in back, medium-size ones in the center, and low-edging types at the front. The neat appearance adds to the geometry of the border.

An informal border may be rectangular or curving; its plantings are less regimented. Plants are intermingled rather than set out in distinct patterns that are repeated at regular intervals. In informal beds plants are not strictly ordered by height, and they can spill over the edges.

Color schemes
In formal borders plants are arranged in specific color groups, which are repeated at regular intervals. Informal borders contain plants in a range of colors. The planting may seem random, but it is as carefully balanced as in a formal border.

Variation in color within one group of plants is more welcome in an informal border than in a formal one. The proportions of colors in an informal border tend to vary, with huge drifts of one shade dotted with small splashes of contrasting color. Many herbaceous perennials are best planted in groups of three or five, depending on their eventual spread, although a few, such as bear's breeches *(Acanthus mollis)*, are large and imposing enough to be grown as individual specimens.

In general, a border that is framed by a fence, wall, or hedge should have a tiered effect — with tall plants set at the back and shorter ones set in front. Variety and informality can be introduced by bringing forward one or two clumps or individual plants of medium height. This arrangement works very well with mid- and late-season plants, which can fill the gaps left by earlier-flowering types. With free-standing borders, the tallest plants should be placed in the center.

Focal points
Any border, formal or informal,

▼ **Summer profusion** Informal drifts of herbaceous perennials, predominantly in shades of pink and red, are held together with scattered stands of spiky, metallic blue hollies *(Eryngium maritimum)*. A background of conifers and a raised urn filled with bright summer bedding plants add a vertical perspective.

▲ **Fall colors** One of the joys of fall is the fleshy-leaved sedum *(Hylotelephium spectabile),* with its large, flattened flower heads that gradually deepen to richer shades. Here, a soft rose form, 'Carmen,' nestles near tall-stemmed blue *Agapanthus* hybrids. The two are complemented by a band of silvery *Artemisia ludoviciana.* In the background New England asters *(Aster novae-angliae* 'Harrington's Pink') contribute more fall color.

◀ **Butterfly plants** While butterflies love the fall-flowering sedums *(above),* in late summer another plant attracts these charming insects: the gray-leaved *Buddleia* 'Lochinch,' with its violet-blue flower spikes, plays generous host to swarms of butterflies. In a small garden, make it a focal point in a mixed border and match it with the pink-flowered tree mallow *(Lavatera olbia)* and the cerise-pink trumpet flowers of *Crinum* x *powellii.*

▶ **Color spots** Bright highlights can be introduced to herbaceous borders with temporary plants. In summer many herbaceous borders lack color after the first, early-summer flush and before later-flowering perennials come into bloom. Here, a miniature, fancy-leaved salmon-pink pelargonium lights up a corner where the cone-shaped flowers of sea hollies *(Eryngium maritimum)* have yet to develop their blue color.

The lime-green flower sprays of lady's mantle *(Alchemilla mollis)* cascade to one side; at the other, a golden-leaved spirea is thrown into clear relief by a potted plant.

▼ **Focal points** Use potted plants where, for example, paving gives way to grass or where lifted spring bulbs have left bare patches in a bed. A group of potted plants creates greater visual impact than does a scattering of individual pots. You can change them or add more pots if flower color is lacking or contrast in shape or form is desired.

Daily watering of potted plants is essential, as is regular deadheading to maintain continuous flowering. At the end of summer, move half-hardy types to a frost-free greenhouse and keep them almost dry during winter.

can be planned around one or more focal points. Provide emphasis with bold foliage, such as that of yuccas or castor beans *(Ricinus),* and include clumps of hostas or similar foliage plants near the front. Use silver and gray leaves, which have a calming influence, to separate one color group from another.

Aim for pleasing color combinations that will continue all through the flowering season. Include perennials, bulbs, and shrubs that will provide fall and winter color. One popular design incorporates blue, pink, and white blooms only. Another possibility is a scheme based on blues, yellows, and creams. For a "hotter" effect, replace the blues with oranges, reds, and purples mixed with gray-leaved foliage plants. Use varying leaf tints for contrast

▲ **Foliage partners** The fragrant plantain lily *(Hosta plantaginea),* with its long-stemmed, glossy green leaves, is a distinctive and beautiful foliage plant. Unlike other hostas, it tolerates full sun, developing its tall spikes of pure white trumpet flowers in late summer and early fall. Here, it supplies magnificent contrast for the small, dark purple leaves of the smoke tree *(Cotinus coggygria* 'Royal Purple').

◀ **Leaf contrasts** Hostas are given plenty of room to show off their impressive leaves in the rich, moisture-retentive soil alongside a pool and in the light shade cast by a flowering crab apple tree. Contrasting in shape, size, and color, their differences are accentuated by young ferns pushing up their feathery fronds.

with cool or hot colors and for accent points.

A single-color flower scheme, such as an all-white border, can be very beautiful, although relying on just one flower color is too limiting for a small garden. Successful one-color borders rely on the shape and texture of foliage, a spot of some other color, supplied perhaps by a single flower of contrasting hue, and a range of tonal variations to keep the monochromatic theme from being an uninspiring color mass.

Borders with a difference
Borders in raised beds can rationalize level changes in a sloped garden, or they can serve as a design feature, perhaps in a flat urban garden. They are much easier to maintain than long borders and have drier root conditions,

ideal for many alpines or hardy succulents. Raised beds and borders can be used for single-color displays, or they can be devoted to plants of a single genus, such as irises, fuchsias, or roses, or to a particular type of plant, such as culinary herbs or ferns.

Narrow or ribbon borders that are planted with parallel rows of colorful annuals, interspersed with bulbs for added height, are excellent for lining paths. Single-color schemes, especially plantings of white, blue, or pink, or silver and gray, can look effective in such narrow beds.

Seasonal groups
In a spacious garden, you can create a different border for each season of the year. Alternatively, you can refurbish a herbaceous border several times a year by

▲ **White for contrast** White flowers introduce an aura of calm and freshness to a herbaceous border; they also help to accentuate other colors and give definition to a planting scheme. The focal point of this combination is a container of single-flowered white petunias topped by white chrysanthemums, with trailing yellow coreopsis at their feet.

lifting plants after they have finished flowering, moving them to a reserve bed, and then replacing them with cultivars that come into bloom later in the season.

However, this option is both labor-intensive and time-consuming. Furthermore, most gardens have no space for reserve beds. It is better to enjoy a spring and summer border, and to try to extend the display into fall or even early winter.

It is a sensible idea to include

evergreen shrubs, perennials, and other plants that provide interest outside the summer months. Early chrysanthemums, dahlias, asters, schizostylises, gladioli, fall-flowering crocuses and colchicums, cyclamens, and lilies can add color to the garden until the first fall frost.

Christmas roses, early-blooming irises, pulmonarias, aconites, camellias, and viburnums offer intermittent color until spring. Then doronicums, bergenias, dicentras, primroses, and lenten roses bloom until early summer.

Bulbs are very valuable for color before summer. Plant small pockets of bare soil with crocuses, snowdrops, winter aconites, and anemones. Mark bare spaces and put in the bulbs as early in the fall as possible. Add annuals, biennials, and potted plants for instant color in early summer.

Border maintenance
Herbaceous borders are more permanent than annual displays, but they still need some renovation. Except for perennials, such as acanthuses and peonies, which resent root disturbance, most plants benefit from being lifted and divided every 3 or 5 years, and some, such as asters, will deteriorate in shape, size, and color unless divided every 3 years.

▲ **Lady's mantle** *Alchemilla mollis* is invaluable to gardeners and flower arrangers because it is ultrahardy (zone 3) and quick to self-seed. Its yellow-green flowers spill over edges and mingle happily with foliage plants. Here, it highlights the orange-scarlet trumpets of a near-evergreen honeysuckle.

Borders alter naturally as shrubs grow and take up more space, and older plants die or are replaced by others. If a new plant appears weak, grows too tall, or clashes with its neighbors in form or color, move it to a better spot in late fall or early spring, while the plant is dormant.

▶ Flowering foliage plants Although hostas are primarily grown for their magnificent leaves, many are also outstanding for their erect spikes of tubular flowers. These range from white through shades of lilac and mauve, and are sometimes fragrant. This handsome group thrives in light shade, where the boldly ribbed hosta leaves contrast with lacy fern fronds, and the pale lilac hosta spikes with fluffy lady's mantle.

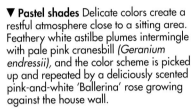

▼ Pastel shades Delicate colors create a restful atmosphere close to a sitting area. Feathery white astilbe plumes intermingle with pale pink cranesbill *(Geranium endressii)*, and the color scheme is picked up and repeated by a deliciously scented pink-and-white 'Ballerina' rose growing against the house wall.

▶ **Bogside companions** In early summer a cultivar of the moisture-loving *Iris chrysographes* raises 2 ft (60 cm) tall stems bearing flowers of such a deep purple color that they appear almost black. Here, the somber tone is lightened with drifts of double golden buttercups *(Ranunculus acris* 'Flore Pleno'). The grasslike iris foliage and the deeply cut leaves of the buttercups are in strong contrast to the ribbed hosta leaves.

◀ **Hosta associates** Hostas are unsurpassed for sheer luxuriance of foliage. *Hosta crispula,* a Japanese species, is one of the finest, forming a dense mass of elongated, heart-shaped ribbed leaves that are dark green with a broad white edge. The leaves are elegantly wavy and ideally suited for massive ground cover. Here, they are seen in late summer fronting a graceful variegated *Fuchsia magellanica* as it droops its scarlet bells over pale mauve hosta spikes.

COLORED COVER

**Groups of ground-cover plants provide
a dense ornamental carpet as
visually exciting as any other combination.**

Well-chosen ground-cover plants are much more than a labor-saving device for suppressing weeds. Many have beautiful flowers, and the best have attractive year-round foliage that can play a key part in any planting scheme. These plants have a wide range that can fit all soils, seasons, and situations.

Most ground-cover plants colonize rapidly or form tight, rounded clumps. Colonizers spread quickly, sending up suckers from a wide-reaching network of roots or rooting from stems that touch the ground. Clump formers, such as hostas, build up more slowly but can still create a compact group of plants that eventually cover the ground.

Weed-proof foliage

Many ground-cover plants have a long and vivid flowering season — moss phlox and aubrieta are outstanding examples. Others,

such as *Cotoneaster dammeri*, carry a handsome crop of berries in fall and winter. But what really makes all these plants invaluable is their foliage.

Evergreens are particularly important in creating ground-cover effects. Ivy, for example, has a huge range of silver and gold variegations, as well as different leaf sizes, textures, and shapes.

Other "evergreens" include plants with silvery gray leaves, which are particularly useful for introducing a lighter area of planting in shady places or as a contrast with conifers or other dark-leaved plants. *Stachys byzantina* is a fine example, and another is *Euonymus fortunei* 'Silver Queen.' Some plants, such as *Gaultheria procumbens,* acquire rich red tones in late summer and fall.

Deciduous ground-cover plants are slightly less effective than evergreens in controlling weeds,

▲ **Creeping cover** The spreading stems of low-growing knotweed *(Polygonum affine)* form a dense carpet of narrow, dark green leaves that turn russet-brown in fall and persist until spring. From midsummer to midfall, the leaf carpet is topped by 8 in (20 cm) tall spikes of deep pink flowers, which make fine companions for blue-flowered asters.

▼ **Woodland carpet** In moist shady soil, arching *Smilacina racemosa* and white-flowered *Trillium grandiflorum* provide a blooming ground cover from midspring to late spring. Their soft colors blend well with bright azaleas.

which can germinate each year before good leaf cover is produced in spring. But they do include some excellent plants, such as lungwort *(Pulmonaria* species) and *Geranium* species, which build up large clumps of splendid leaves.

Open, sunny sites
In open, sunny areas ground-cover plants can provide attractive background planting. They can also merit a place of their own because of their flowers, foliage, and ease of care. Cranesbills *(Geranium),* a large and beautiful group of ornamental plants, are valuable for their notched and divided leaves. The foliage dies in fall but reappears in early spring or midspring to form close cover.

Viola cornuta, a plant with attractive light green leaves and violet or white flowers produced abundantly over a long period, is perfect as a foil for more showy plants. The blue-flowered form provides one of the best underplantings for beds of bush roses.

Not all open, sunny positions are easy to plant, since they often lack moisture. But many ground-cover plants thrive even in dry soils. *Ballota pseudodictamnus,* catmint *(Nepeta × faassenii), Artemisia stellerana,* and lavender cotton *(Santolina chamaecyparissus)* are all ideal for dry and sunny sites.

Heaths and heathers like acid soil, although *Erica carnea* tolerates slightly alkaline soil. A mixture of heathers offers a long flowering season; the color of the foliage — and even of the dead blooms — extends their interest.

Heavily shaded sites
Ivy is one of the most successful plants for siting beneath trees, as there is an abundance of choice in leaf color and shape. Irish ivy *(Hedera helix* 'Hibernica') is particularly good, rapidly forming a dense cover. The silver and golden variegated forms of the common ivy *(H. helix)* are especially attractive; these ivies introduce a valuable element of color into areas of deep shade.

Also ideal for the area beneath trees is the yellow dead nettle *(Lamium galeobdolon* 'Variegatum'), with its beautifully marbled leaves. However, it grows rampantly and must be prevented from spreading, or it will smother more delicate neighbors.

Light or dappled shade
There are many plants to choose from, but few can match hostas for magnificent foliage. Hostas like a humus-rich soil and tolerate dry soil; they are thus ideal for planting under trees.

Another worthy plant is lady's mantle *(Alchemilla mollis).* This flourishes in sun and light shade, rapidly developing mounds of large, velvety leaves and a froth of greenish-yellow flowers during spring. It is a prolific self-seeder, whose knack of fitting in between other plants makes the garden appear full to overflowing.

▼ **Cottage-garden charm** Old-fashioned favorites like blue-flowered lavender and silvery lavender cotton *(Santolina chamaecyparissus)* form spreading mounds of fragrant, eye-catching cover.

▲ **Shady companions** Bugle *(Ajuga reptans)* clothes the ground with rosettes of evergreen leaves, dark purple in the form 'Atropurpurea.' It thrives in shady sites and bears blue flowers in summer. Creeping Jenny *(Lysimachia nummularia)* flourishes in similar conditions and brightens the bugle foliage with its yellow flowers.

▶ **Frontline shrubs** Small, shrubby potentillas *(Potentilla fruticosa)* provide good weed-smothering cover in large shrub borders and are almost in permanent bloom from early summer until the fall frosts. The yellow-flowered 'Elizabeth' and the smaller, orange-colored 'Tangerine' complement the semievergreen *Hypericum* x *inodorum* 'Elstead,' resplendent in late summer with clusters of scarlet berries.

▲ **Spotted lungwort** Partial shade and moist soil suit the lungworts, which spread to form a distinctive ground cover, marbled with silver in the species *Pulmonaria saccharata*. Here, the violet-blue flowers look stunning beneath the arching branches of a white-flowered pearlbush, *Exochorda racemosa*.

▲ **Spring color** The dainty wake-robin *(Trillium grandiflorum)* forms spreading clumps in moist shady sites, opening its three-petaled flowers in spring. White at first, they later become flushed with pink to match the developing chestnutlike leaves of coppery *Rodgersia podophylla*.

▼ **Shady site** In light and dense shade, combine the evergreen, low-growing Japanese spurge *(Pachysandra terminalis)* with upright stands of golden green ostrich ferns *(Matteuccia struthiopteris)*. Japanese spurge will continue to provide good ground cover in fall and winter.

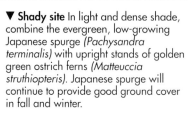

▶ **Colorful bugles** The perennial bugle *(Ajuga reptans)* is invasive by nature and quickly covers any bare soil with its attractive leaf rosettes and small blue flower spikes. The cultivar 'Burgundy Glow,' in leaf colors that span metallic bronze, pink, and cream, highlights the white-edged, ribbed leaves of *Hosta* 'Thomas Hogg.'

▼ **Lady's mantle** In sun or light shade north to zone 4, lady's mantle *(Alchemilla mollis)* spreads to form mounds of pale green, hairy palmate leaves. They are topped during summer by billowing sprays of delicate lime-green blooms, invaluable for garden decoration and flower arrangements. The plants self-seed and colonize readily. Unwanted seedlings should be rooted out.

▲ **Spotted dead nettle** Near-evergreen in all but the severest of winters, the spotted dead nettle *(Lamium maculatum* 'Beacon Silver') invades nooks and odd corners, where it lays an ever-increasing carpet of heart-shaped green leaves flecked with silver. The hooded purple flowers appear in late spring and then sporadically until the frost. To contain the plants and to keep them neat, shear off the flower heads once the first flush of bloom has ended.

▲ **Succulent cover** Many types of alpine plants carpet soil and stones in the rock garden with ever-spreading leaf rosettes, mats, and low mounds. Here, clumps of green- and purple-leaved houseleeks *(Sempervivum tectorum)* creep among mats of silvery *Raoulia* and the linear gray-green foliage of *Gypsophila repens.*

A yellow carpet of stonecrop *(Sedum acre)* ripples through the leaf cover like a pool of sunlight.

◄ **Fall colors** The deep purple-red fleshy leaves of a stonecrop *(Sedum)* are overlaid with a bloom in the cultivar 'Maximum Atropurpureum.' The plant spreads to form clumps that are topped in early fall with purple-pink flower heads. In this handsome late-summer association, the purple color is subdued by stately cream-white spikes of a hybrid red-hot poker *(Kniphofia)* and the yellow-green froth of ground-hugging lady's mantle *(Alchemilla mollis).*

DECORATING WITH BULBS

**With the right choice of bulbs, a garden
can come to life in fall and winter, in addition to
offering a spring and summer display.**

Tulips, hyacinths, and daffodils are by far the most popular bulbs, and they are traditional spring features in almost every garden. But bulbs can also provide flowers in summer, fall, and — in mild-weather regions — winter. Fall-flowering crocuses, cyclamens, and nerines, for example, can brighten a garden once herbaceous perennials finish. Early-flowering irises, snowdrops, and aconites bloom even before the winter snow has fully melted; and lilies, including the beautiful, easy-to-grow *Lilium regale,* add beauty and scent to summer.

Bulbs and corms are useful even in a tiny garden. Many need only planting and occasional lifting and dividing. Some, such as snowdrops and crocuses, are completely care-free, and naturalize by seed and bulblet into attractive clumps or drifts.

Compared with herbaceous perennials, dormant bulbs are clean to handle and cheap to buy. Bulb catalogs often offer discounts for bulk orders, especially for types used in mass planting.

▶ **Grape hyacinth** Undemanding and easy to grow, the grape hyacinth *(Muscari armeniacum)* is ideal for naturalizing in a sunny site. Its cheerful blue flower spikes appear in early spring.

▼ **Fall crocuses** Welcome for its startling splashes of color, *Colchicum speciosum* produces only lush, coarse foliage in spring; the splendid violet goblets of bloom appear by themselves in the fall.

Larger garden centers offer popular types by the basketful — again at attractive prices.

Unlike most seeds, bulbs are easy to handle and can be placed exactly where you want them. Unless you do something drastically wrong, as many bulbs as you plant will flower, at least for the first year. Many bulbs are long-lived, so that they or their progeny carry on year after year. It is not uncommon for bulbs to continue blooming long after garden and house have disappeared.

The choice is virtually unlimited. Flower colors vary from brilliant white to subtle shades and pastels, with bicolored and multicolored flowers in soft or quite startling combinations. The flower can take the shape of a star, daisy, trumpet, cup, or goblet; it can be single or double; held upright or gracefully nodding; carried singly, in spikes, or in many-flowered clusters.

Heights range from the diminutive, ground-carpeting *Anemone blanda*, a few inches high, to giant lilies *(Cardiocrinum giganteum)* 8 ft (2.4 m) tall, with every variation in between. Flower sizes, too, extend from modest little grape hyacinths to large and showy hybrid gladioli. It's always worth studying bulb catalogs; many flamboyant hybrids have been bred from their smaller, more graceful species relatives, which are just as easy to grow.

There are flowering bulbs for sun and for shade; for hot, dry conditions and waterlogged bogs; for acid and alkaline soils, and for fertile and poor soils. Flamboyant exotics such as the pineapple lily *(Eucomis bicolor)* and the heavily scented ginger lily *(Hedychium)* will flourish in southern and southwestern gardens. If lifted and stored each winter, they will do well in northern gardens, too.

Bulbous plants
A bulb is an organ for storing food and water, and it allows a plant to remain dormant for a long time. Structurally, a bulb is a swollen leaf base holding an embryo bud; daffodils, tulips, and onions are true bulbs.

Other storage organs, such as iris rhizomes, gladiolus corms, and cyclamen tubers, are basically swollen stems or roots, but in purpose and treatment, they are similar to bulbs. For convenience, all are referred to as bulbs here.

In the garden bulbs from the lily, iris, and amaryllis families dominate the scene, providing all-time favorites as well as enchantingly beautiful but less well-known flowers.

Growing bulbs
While a few bulbs, such as arums, have attractive foliage and some, such as *Iris foetidissima*, have beautiful seedpods, the majority are grown for their flowers.

Because modern cultivars produce perfectly uniform, virtually identical plants, bulbs are popular for formal spring bedding displays. Straight-stemmed, early single tulips and Dutch hyacinths, for example, are often interplanted with polyanthuses or forget-me-nots.

Grown informally, bulbs have many uses, from providing pockets of color in a rock garden, to brightening up mixed beds until the arrival of summer's herbaceous perennial colors. Early-flowering bulbs are very effective as underplanting, making up for the lack of color and interest in dormant deciduous shrubs.

Bulbs planted with late-leafing

▼ **Bluebell glade** In late spring the deep blue of bluebells *(Hyacinthoides non-scripta)* blends delightfully with the cool, fresh green of unfolding blue-flowered *Hosta* 'Honeybells.'

◀ **Bedding tulips** Hundreds of tulip cultivars are available, differing in size, shape, and color and spanning a flowering season of several months. Highly decorative types, like the double late tulip 'Peach Blossom,' are most effective when massed in beds of their own kind. After flowering, they should be lifted, dried off, and stored until being replanted in late fall.

▼ **Summer bulb** The brightly colored Peruvian lily (*Alstroemeria ligtu* 'Hybrids') adds an exotic touch to the summer garden. It needs good soil, sun, and a sheltered site in which it can be left undisturbed for years.

perennials and shrubs, such as Japanese anemones and hardy hibiscues, give double the color in relation to the space.

Spring bulbs can work in tandem with summer bedding, filling beds with color until half-hardy annuals and perennials such as pelargoniums, petunias, and begonias come into bloom.

Daffodils, crocuses, bluebells, snowdrops, as well as low-growing anemones and fritillaries are ideal for naturalizing, and a relatively small investment gives increasing returns every year. Crocuses and fritillaries are usually naturalized in grass, while snowdrops are perfect for growing under and around deciduous hedges as well as in grass. Bluebells and daffodils, being taller, are best naturalized in meadow grass or light woodland conditions — the latter is also excellent for anemones.

With the exception of bluebells, most bulbs will grow happily in containers: place dwarf bulbs in troughs or pans; larger bulbs in pots, tubs, urns, and window boxes. Raised beds are essentially large-scale containers, and bulbs, especially those liking good drainage, thrive there.

Aftercare of bulbs

Some bulbs, such as tulips, degenerate if left in the ground year after year. They produce a number of bulblets, masses of foliage, and fewer and smaller flowers. To prevent this, lift, store, and replant

◀ **Winter joy** Few plants give as much pleasure as the little snowdrop *(Galanthus nivalis)* as it pushes its tender-green tips through the bare soil of late winter or very early spring. Its pure white, gracefully nodding bells pronounce that life in the garden is about to reawaken, in spite of forbidding cold weather.

▼ **Late spring** Certain classic bedding designs never go out of style. Tall-stemmed tulips and multicolored, sweetly scented wallflowers are a time-honored tradition that seems fresh every spring.

▲ **Pink companions** In early summer ornamental onions *(Allium aflatunense)* raise their deep pink globes on tall stems above mat-forming snakeweed *(Polygonum bistorta* 'Superbum') with its clear pink flower spikes. They are accompanied by the lush foliage of lady's mantle *(Alchemilla mollis)*, which has not yet bloomed.

▶ **Winter cheer** A golden cascade of late-winter-flowering jasmine *(Jasminum nudiflorum)* offsets the showy blue-flowered *Iris histrioides* which sparkles among such other early-flowering bulbs as golden *Crocus flavus*, carmine-pink *Cyclamen coum*, and pure white snowdrops.

annually. Dutch hyacinths can be lifted, but if left to naturalize (through zone 5) they have smaller, though sweet-scented, flowers.

Half-hardy bulbs, such as large-flowered gladioli, need annual lifting and storing to protect them from frost damage. Alternatively, you can select one of the smaller-flowered species, such as *Gladio-* *lus byzantinus,* which is hardy to zone 5.

Many tall-flowering bulbs, such as gladioli, should be staked to avoid appearing ungainly. However, bare-stemmed, tall-flowering bulbs, such as alliums and lilies, should be planted where they can support themselves on shrubs or perennials.

▼ **Woodland sites** Ideal to plant under shrubs and trees, *Cyclamen hederifolium* (hardy to zone 7) will unfold a floral carpet from late summer until fall when sited in soil rich in leaf mold and sheltered from hot sun and strong winds. The beautiful white, pale pink, and mauve flowers are accompanied by deep green heart-shaped leaves with silvery markings.

PARTNERS FOR SPRING BULBS

**Daffodils and tulips are among the best-loved bulbs.
Together with other spring bulbs, they bring color to the
garden for several months.**

Bulbs are deservedly popular. Their flowers come in strikingly beautiful colors and an enormous variety of shapes. In height, they range from miniatures for the rock garden, raised beds, and troughs to the 3 ft (90 cm) tall stately crown imperials for the rear of herbaceous borders.

Such diversity provides a wide scope for associations with other bulbous plants or with trees, shrubs, and other plants.

Spring is the time for crocuses, anemones, trilliums, scillas, daffodils, narcissi, hyacinths, fritillaries, and tulips to be grown in containers and window boxes, naturalized in grass, and bedded in formal displays.

In very early spring, the days are brightened with snowdrops, *Cyclamen coum,* winter aconites *(Eranthis hyemalis),* and silver-blue scillas. Their pastel colors provide a taste of the warmer weather that is to come beneath the bare branches of wintersweet *(Chimonanthus praecox).* The lime-green flowers and evergreen foliage of *Helleborus foetidus* add height and leafy interest.

By midspring, sturdy-stemmed and sweet-scented hyacinths enter the picture. They can form the basis of many contrasting or harmonious bedding plans partnered with cottage tulips, pansies, and primroses, for example.

Fritillaries, too, arrive by midspring, including the pretty snake's-head *(Fritillaria meleagris),* which is equally at home in meadow grass or an undisturbed corner of the border. Its checkered purple bells seem graceful nodding over a carpet of forget-me-nots and look stunning with tall, pink and purple lenten roses *(Helleborus orientalis).*

The spectacular crown imperial *(Fritillaria imperalis),* in lovely shades of yellow, orange, and scarlet, can hold court over drifts of cream-flowered trout lilies *(Erythronium* 'White Beauty') or white-flowered narcissi. Alternatively, plant a luxurious carpet of mauve-flowered *Viola labradorica* 'Purple Leaf' interspersed with miniature yellow-and-white *Tulipa tarda* at their feet.

Partners for daffodils
Daffodils and other narcissi raise their cheerful yellow and white flowers year after year, celebrating the arrival of spring in a variety of garden situations.

▼ **Picture of spring** Large-cupped narcissi and bright, sturdy-stemmed Darwin hybrid tulips mix easily in midspring. They are fronted by yellow *Aurinia saxatilis* and white arabis.

▲ **Color contrasts** The sweetly scented, multiflowered tazetta narcissus 'Geranium' blooms in late spring. Its bright orange-scarlet cups are surrounded by pure white petals. Planted in drifts beneath a deciduous tree, it is partnered by elegant lily-flowered 'Aladdin' tulips. Their showy, pointed carmine goblets, edged with gold, offer stunning contrasts in form and color to the softer, gently weaving narcissi.

▶ **Spring meadow** Jostling in tall grass around a moss-covered tree trunk, cheerful spring bulbs revel in each other's company. Beautifully proportioned, long-trumpeted cyclamineus narcissi lean protectively over pure white *Anemone apennina* and miniature golden suns of the lesser celandine *(Ranunculus ficaria)*. Scattered in the grass are the charming purple-checkered bells of snake's-head fritillary *(Fritillaria meleagris)*, which often produce white seedlings when left to colonize.

◄ **Hoop petticoats** The dainty hoop petticoat *(Narcissus bulbocodium)* is one of the first narcissi to flower. Unlike other narcissi, it often produces its yellow petticoats in winter snow. This imitation alpine meadow is backed by the precocious spring heath *(Erica carnea)* and other narcissi, which include the 1 ft (30 cm) tall Tenby daffodil *(Narcissus pseudonarcissus obvallaris),* with golden frilly-edged trumpets, and the cyclamineus narcissus 'Jack Snipe,' with creamy white petals and a primrose cup.

As a complement to the heaths, rose-purple dog's-tooth violets *(Erythronium dens-canis)* nod their elegant flowers among the yellow and green.

▲ **'February Gold'** Rarely flowering quite as early as its name would suggest, the cyclamineus narcissus 'February Gold' with its narrow trumpets and backswept petals, is perfect for naturalizing in moist, grassy places with dappled shade.

In acid soil its brilliant yellow trumpets combine beautifully with the deciduous *Rhododendron mucronulatum,* which displays rose-purple flowers on bare branches. Patches of bright blue, white-eyed glory-of-the-snow *(Chionodoxa luciliae)* are threaded through the narcissi clumps for subtle contrast.

▲ **Midspring splendor** Clumps of sturdy trumpet daffodils spread pools of sunlight over roughly mowed grass. They colonize steadily in the dappled shade of an ornamental cherry tree, whose slender branches of pale pink blossoms are beginning to droop downward. Later, the fully clothed branches will help to draw the eye away from the untidy leaves of the dying daffodils.

▶ **Study in yellow** An early spring pairing of yellow and green is centered around the evergreen Oregon grape *(Mahonia aquifolium)*. The glossy hollylike leaf clusters, which often turn red in fall, are surmounted by dense clusters of yellow flower spikes, which brighten shady sites. To the rear, the elegant leafless tracery of winter hazel *(Corylopsis willmottiae)* is hung with pale yellow catkins, while in the foreground trumpets of the common daffodil *(Narcissus pseudonarcissus)* nod above the silver-marbled leaves of fall-flowering *Cyclamen hederifolium.*

Sturdy trumpet daffodils, such as 'Golden Harvest' and 'Mount Hood,' are ideal for containers, combined with pansies and hyacinths, for example.

On a larger scale, a formal bed can have clumps of trumpet daffodils or large-cupped narcissi and a range of stiffly upright tulips. And for a different flower shape, graceful cyclamineus narcissi with backswept petals are dainty traditional partners for the neat blue grape hyacinth.

Plant daffodils and narcissi between shrubs in mixed borders, where, after blossoming, their dying foliage will be hidden by plants that come into leaf later. Or use ground-cover plants with ornamental foliage to camouflage the narcissi's browning leaves. Try silver variegated forms of *Lamium maculatum* and bronze, pink, and yellow bugle (*Ajuga reptans* 'Multicoloris'). White daffodils are a superb contrast for the purplish foliage of *A. reptans*

'Atropurpurea' or for the mauve blooms and purple leaves of *Viola labradorica* 'Purple Leaf.'

To many people, daffodils and narcissi look best planted in drifts and naturalized in grass among the roots of deciduous trees and shrubs, which come into full leaf as the bulbs finish blooming. Leave space between the groups to plant cobalt-blue, white-edged *Muscari armeniacum*; dog's-tooth violet (*Erythronium dens-canis*), snake's-head fritillary (*Fritillaria meleagris*), deep blue *Anemone apennina;* and the yellowish-gold Dutch crocuses, which flourish in light shade and are excellent for naturalizing in grass.

Partners for tulips

Tulips set alone are very impressive, but their impact is even greater when they are placed with plants of contrasting or harmonious colors.

Perhaps the most classic partners for tulips are forget-me-nots

(*Myosotis sylvatica*) and wallflowers (*Erysimum cheiri*). Use *Myosotis* 'Royal Blue' with tall lemon-yellow or pink tulips.

Wallflowers look best in a mass of one color. You can also contrast *Erysimum* 'Primrose Bedder' and 'Cloth of Gold' with the maroon tulip 'Queen of the Night' and *Erysimum* 'Blood Red' with white, orange, or flame-hued tulips.

In mixed borders, purple honesty (*Lunaria annua*) mixes well with 'Golden Apeldoorn' tulips, while white honesty 'Alba' is a stark contrast to maroon-black tulip goblets. For harmony, use the golden daisies of *Doronicum* 'Madame Mason' with yellow tulips, and add some blue grape hyacinths (*Muscari*) for extra splashes of color.

▼ **Leaf foil** Maroon-spotted leaves are characteristic of the Greigii hybrid tulips. Blooming in midspring, they are partnered here with striped *Phalaris arundinacea* 'Picta.'

▲ **Rock garden tulips** The delightful little *Tulipa tarda*, only 4 in (10 cm) high, is ideal for pockets of well-drained, gritty soil in a sunny rock garden. In bright sun, up to five flowers on each stem open out to form white, yellow-centered stars. This tulip flowers in late spring at the same time as the pasqueflower *(Pulsatilla vulgaris)*, with its elegant, finely divided foliage and rich purple-blue flowers. A neutral background, such as greenish-gray rosemary, sets both off to perfection.

▶ **Tulip partners** Kaufmanniana hybrid tulips, sometimes known as water-lily tulips, open wide in early-spring sunshine to reveal their pointed petals, usually flushed with a contrasting color. Virginia bluebells *(Mertensia virginica)*, with their drooping clusters of pure blue flowers, make admirable companions.

▼ **Blue and yellow** This formal bedding scheme for late spring is based on forget-me-nots, with late-flowering yellow and creamy white tulips rising from waves of luxuriant bright blue *Myosotis sylvatica.* The blue-and-yellow theme is continued with an edging of a compact indigo-blue *Myosotis* cultivar, 'Blue Ball,' broken dramatically by golden *Aurinia saxatilis* 'Citrinum.'

▶ **Early spring** The Kaufmanniana hybrid tulip 'The First' is aptly named, for this group flowers before any other tulips. Rarely more than 10 in (25 cm) high, it is at home in the rock garden and raised beds. Here, it opens its ivory-white, red-flushed flowers wide above the yellow blooms of evergreen, mat-forming spring cinquefoil *(Potentilla tabernaemontani).*

▶ **Gold on gold** The young orange-red leaves of the dwarf shrub *Spiraea japonica* 'Goldflame' form a harmonious background for tall, stiff-stemmed Darwin hybrid tulips. 'Beauty of Apeldoorn' flowers in midspring to late spring, with distinctive oval-shaped flowers of golden-yellow flushed with soft orange. The cool yellow flower heads of *Euphorbia polychroma* complete the sunny picture.

▲ **Lily flowers** Pansies are traditional partners for tulips, contrasting with them in height, shape, and color. In this bedding scheme, cultivars of *Viola* x *wittrockiana* in sumptuous regal hues pay homage to stately lily-flowered tulips. Flowering in midspring and late spring, these graceful tulips have waisted flowers with long, pointed, and often bicolored petals.

◄ **Symphony in red** The typical late-flowering tulip is goblet- or oval-shaped and borne on strong, stiff stems. Many Darwin hybrid tulips are bicolored, while others come in single shades that accentuate their waxen beauty. Here, cerise-red tulips look spectacular with deep pink Russell lupines, their different shapes clearly highlighted.

SUMMER-FLOWERING BULBS

**The magnificent blooms of lilies and irises are
some of the most beautiful summer flowers and the
center of attention in many partnerships.**

Many bulbous plants can be included in herbaceous and mixed borders. For instance, the Peruvian lily (*Alstroemeria ligtu* 'Hybrids') in sunset colors of pink, apricot, yellow-orange, and red is stunning surrounded by blue delphiniums and yellow loosestrife (*Lysimachia punctata*).

In late summer the blue African lilies (*Agapanthus* 'Headbourne Hybrids') combine well with the flat, yellow flower heads of *Achillea* 'Coronation Gold'; or for striking contrast, add the bold spikes of red-hot poker (*Kniphofia*), perhaps with a foreground planting of silvery *Stachys byzantina*. Also flowering in late summer are the Kaffir lilies (*Schizostylis coccinea*); their exotic scarlet flower spikes look charming with clusters of powder-blue or cream-white New York asters (*Aster novi-belgii*).

Partners for irises

Irises bridge the gap between spring and summer. Some species, *Iris cristata* for example, bloom only in spring; others, such as the Japanese iris (*I. kaempferi*), bloom in summer. Bearded and Louisiana irises straddle the spring and summer seasons.

Whatever their blooming season, irises' flat fans or upright grassy spears of tapering leaves and their strong-stemmed, distinctive flowers make them a delight in the garden. Choosing partners with care can enhance these striking plants with their wide color range and many forms.

Some irises are rare and difficult to grow, but in the right conditions most give little trouble. Flag irises (*Iris × germanica*), for instance, are easy to grow. A background of shrubs is ideal for them — but they should not be in too much shade. The pink flowers and variegated foliage of *Weigela*

▶ **Summer glory** Elegant *Iris sanguinea* forms 1½ ft (45 cm) tall clumps of narrow, dark green foliage. Its creamy yellow flowers calm the exuberance of pink and cerise old-fashioned roses.

▼ **Delicate coloring** A breathtaking early-summer group has the frost-sensitive, mallowlike *Abutilon vitifolium* as its center. The pale purple flowers of this shrub are complemented by pale blue *Iris pallida* 'Dalmatica' above gray-green leaf fans. Yellow tree lupines (*Lupinus arboreus*) unite the colors.

▶ **Bog garden iris** Flowering in early summer and midsummer, the deep purple blooms of 2 ft (60 cm) tall *Iris laevigata* float like exotic butterflies among lush stands of ferns. Astilbes also thrive in boggy conditions, and their emerging feathery sprays delay their flower displays until the irises have faded.

▶ **Tricolor scheme** Elegant *Iris sibirica* raises its blue flowers against a froth of creamy white 'Nevada' roses. Black-eyed *Geranium psilostemon* adds points of deep magenta-pink.

▲ **Waving the flag** Cottage-garden flowers — pale pink campion *(Silene dioica)* in the foreground and scented pink-and-white dame's violets *(Hesperis matronalis)* — weave a tapestry of flowers and foliage in late spring. Held regally above them are the spectacular white-bearded, purple blooms of the flag iris *(Iris x germanica)*.

◀ **Water irises** The yellow-flowered *Iris pseudacorus* will reach a height of 5 ft (1.5 m) in garden pools and the marshy ground by streams. Another true water iris, the shorter lavender-blue *I. laevigata*, makes a suitable companion for early-summer color. The swordlike foliage of both plants contrasts superbly with the massive leaves of western skunk cabbage *(Lysichiton americanus)* in the background.

▲ **Japanese floral art** The flamboyant yet delicate iris is popular in traditional Japanese floral decorations, featuring frequently as one of the three elements that are used in ikebana arrangements.

The planting shown here emphasizes the fragile quality of the Japanese iris (*I. kaempferi*). Available in blue, purple, pink, lavender, and white, some forms are bicolored, while others are single hued; still others are netted with white or colored veins.

Mauve and white astilbe plumes reflect the colors of the Japanese iris blooms. Both plants enjoy the same conditions — moist, neutral to acid soil and sun.

◄ **Veiled in white** The tall bearded irises begin flowering in late spring, but bloom on into early summer, especially in cooler, northern regions. The sword-shaped foliage contrasts well with clumps of large-leaved bluish-green *Hosta sieboldiana*. As a background to both, the European cranberry (*Viburnum opulus*) drapes its white flowers amid green maplelike leaves.

florida 'Variegata' make a charming background for pale blue cultivars, while the wine-purple foliage of the smoke tree *(Cotinus coggygria* 'Royal Purple') is a dramatic setting for white forms.

In a mixed border, blue cultivars of the taller bulbous Dutch, Spanish, and English irises are nicely enhanced by an edging of *Anthemis punctata cupaniana,* with its white, yellow-centered daisy flowers and gray foliage.

The soft blue *Iris pallida* 'Dalmatica' is an unusual but effective match for another bulbous plant, the 10 in (25 cm) high ornamental onion *(Allium karataviense)* with its greenish-white, purple-flushed flower globes and striking foliage of broad, dark green leaves tinted with purple.

A moist border is the perfect place for *I. sibirica.* The dark flowers look well with the white-edged leaves of *Hosta crispula.* At the waterside *I. kaempferi* and *I. laevigata* are natural partners for moisture-loving rodgersia, astilbe, and candelabra primulas.

Lily companions

Lilies are magnificent, stately plants with dramatic flowers and fine foliage. Alkaline-hating species are often planted in sunny clearings among rhododendrons and azaleas, whose foliage forms a handsome background. But provided they are not crowded out by other plants, lilies can be used successfully in mixed borders.

A group of 3-4 ft (90-120 cm) tall *Lilium pyrenaicum,* their stems thickly set with narrow leaves and yellow Turk's-cap flowers, makes a lovely picture against a background of golden variegated *Elaeagnus pungens* 'Maculata,' with the yellow-edged foliage of *Hosta fortunei* 'Aureomarginata' in front.

The pure white trumpets of alkaline-tolerant, sun-loving *Lilium candidum* look wonderful with the burgundy-purple old garden rose 'Reine des Violettes.' Alternatively, in partial shade, place graceful ferns and the purple-pink *Lilium martagon* with the pinkish white flowers of *Astrantia major.*

Orange-red Asiatic hybrids look stunning with the blues of delphiniums, *Campanula lactiflora,* the hardy geranium 'Johnson's Blue,' and *Nepeta.*

Scented *Lilium regale* mixes

well with yellow- and buff-flowered verbascums and with *Artemisia ludoviciana* 'Silver King,' whose silver foliage acts as a foil to the wine-purple shading on white lily trumpets. Or, for late summer, plant apricot-orange *Lilium henryi* with purple-leaved *Atriplex hortensis* 'Rubra.'

▼ **Asiatic lily hybrids** The brightly colored, hardy Asiatic hybrids are some of the easiest lilies to grow. The upward-facing large blooms are carried in clusters in summer on strong leafy stems and are excellent for cutting. Colors range through shades of yellow, orange, and red, sometimes spotted with black.

▲ **Regal lilies** In the warmth and shelter of a sunny wall, graceful regal lilies *(Lilium regale)* preside over blue-flowered *Agapanthus* 'Headbourne Hybrids.' Wine-red in bud, the scented lily clusters open to pure white trumpets that flare back to reveal golden throats and yellow stamens, a color picked up by the daisy flowers of the silvery gray *Senecio* at the front of the garden bed.

◄ **Summer brides** For thousands of years the lily has been associated with sanctity and purity. It appears in Greek and Roman mythology and in Christian history. It was commonly featured in medieval paintings, and is the national emblem of France. Yet in spite of all the honors heaped upon it, the regal lily *(Lilium regale)* flourishes in the most ordinary of gardens. It trumpets its wax-white blooms at the height of summer, in the company of orange-pink *Alstroemeria ligtu* 'Hybrids' and veiled in the soft white foil of baby's breath.

◀ **Lilies by other names** The South African pineapple lily (*Eucomis* species) takes its common name from the tuft of pineapple-like bracts at the top of the sturdy flower stem. Flowering greenish white in late summer, it contrasts in color and form with the elegant *Lilium speciosum*, whose fragrant flowers are heavily shaded with crimson on the backswept petals. *Eucomis* will not survive winters north of zone 7, and must be lifted in fall to overwinter in a frost-free greenhouse or plant room. Still, given the exotic look it gives to a bed or border, ambitious gardeners will find this plant worth the trouble.

▼ **Pure enchantment** The golden red 'Enchantment' lily is one of the most popular of the Asiatic hybrids. Vigorous and fully hardy, it produces its bright clusters of outward-facing blooms, each up to 6 in (15 cm) wide, in mid-summer year after year. It flourishes in full sun, with some shade over the root area, here provided by a mini forest of evergreen, pale blue lavender (*Lavandula angustifolia*).

◄ **Madonna lily** Named after the Virgin Mary and depicted in innumerable religious paintings, the Madonna lily *(Lilium candidum)* has been in cultivation for thousands of years. Hardy through zone 5, if planted in ordinary soil and full sun it will bloom in early summer. The fragrant funnel-shaped flowers are pure white with golden centers, and combine particularly well with gray- or purple-leaved herbs and shrubs. Here, the smoke tree *(Cotinus coggygria* 'Royal Purple') makes a dramatic backdrop for the lilies. Later, their place will be taken by the mauve-tinted, white flowers of *Clematis viticella* 'Alba' scrambling through the shrub.

▼ **Favorite friends** Roses and lilies form classic partnerships, as their main flowering season in midsummer coincides. Good pairings use colors that blend harmoniously without detracting from each other. Here, palest yellow roses take on luster from orange-red Asiatic hybrid lilies, whose flamboyance is toned down by the coolness of the roses.

PORTABLE PARTNERS

Plants in pots and containers increase the opportunities for colorful partnerships and make it easier to cultivate difficult plants.

There are many advantages to growing plants in pots, whatever the size and layout of your garden. In some cases, the special needs of a plant can be met only by confining it to a pot. In other cases, container growing makes caring for plants easier. You can also use plants in pots to conceal eyesores, or move them around like stage props, to create a series of ever-changing garden pictures.

Garden limitations
If you have a balcony, courtyard, or roof garden, growing plants in pots is almost the only option. (Overhanging climbing plants is the only other practical choice.) Concrete areas outside urban basement apartments are also container gardens from necessity. But those that are well planned can be so leafy and flowery that the pots are not noticeable.

Window boxes, pots on a wall, and hanging baskets are often the only claim to a garden for apartment dwellers. Fortunately, plant breeders and garden centers have responded to the growing demand by offering an ever-increasing range of colorful scaled-down plants that are perfect for container growing.

Provided you use sterilized potting soil — not garden soil — weeds and soil pests are all but eliminated in container gardening, though the odd sow bug may creep in through drainage holes.

Plants in containers are more

▼ **Color step by step** A procession of container-grown annuals and bedding plants turns a flight of steps into a cascade of color. Annuals planted in the concrete-block walls create unity.

▲ **Spring garden** A stylish window box always attracts attention. Permanent features like dwarf conifers can be enlivened with spring bulbs and dwarf cinerarias and in summer with colorful annuals.

◄ **Color coordinates** Cool white and yellow annuals echo the colors of the trellis and seating to form an enchanting transition to the garden.

▶ **Specimen plants** A spiky-leaved dracaena underplanted with pelargoniums and silvery helichrysums creates an instant focal point.

easily relocated than their flower bed counterparts — a consideration if you might move. People become attached to their plants, but it can be difficult to uproot prized specimens. Potted plants can be transported with the furniture, giving a new home an instant feeling of welcome.

Cultural needs

Some popular summer plants — tender fuchsias, pelargoniums, and wax begonias — need winter protection. These can be bedded out in late spring and potted up in fall to overwinter indoors, but if they are in pots, it is easier to move them in or out as needed.

Some alpine plants tolerate low winter temperatures but not the

the garden for an outdoor party, using pots of colorful plants.

Although some pots have no inherent beauty, many terra-cotta, wood, fiberglass, stone, or concrete containers are attractive in their own right and contrast well with plants.

Wide, flat-topped walls, both retaining and freestanding ones, can be enhanced by a collection of pot-grown plants. If you set dwarf or alpine plants in wall-mounted pots, you can enjoy their beauty at close quarters without having to stoop to ground level. Provided a path is wide enough, a row of pots can be used as edging or, if width allows, to line garden steps on one or both sides. One huge pot placed at the end of a path, or at the junction of a flower bed and lawn, makes an attractive marker for boundary and level changes. A pair of matching pots placed on either side of a gate or doorway reinforces symmetry and lends an air of formal dignity to the most ordinary entrance.

Plant-filled pots can conceal as well as enhance: a manhole cover, broken paving slab, bathroom window, or ugly bit of wall can completely disappear beneath or behind potted plants.

Choosing short-term plants

Annuals are ideal plants for pots, and are available ready grown, so you can have instant color from late spring until midfall. Spring-flowering biennials, such as wallflowers, forget-me-nots, double daisies, and Canterbury bells, are also good container plants. Some types, such as wallflowers, have small root systems compared to their top growth, so they put on a good display even in small pots.

Bulbs, such as tulips, daffodils, hyacinths, and grape hyacinths, are delightful for potted spring color. With biennials and spring bulbs, it is best to buy and plant them in fall. They can also be bought in flower in spring for planting out, though they are much more expensive then, and you forfeit the pleasure of watching them grow and develop. The same is true for winter-flowering irises, which should be planted in early fall. Pots of summer-flowering lilies offer fragrance as well as magnificent blooms — either plant them while dormant or buy them in flower for instant display.

Herbaceous perennials, such as

wet soil and damp atmosphere that go with them. These, too, are best grown in pots or in special shallow alpine pans and overwintered in an unheated greenhouse.

You may yearn to grow azaleas, rhododendrons, camellias, and summer-flowering heathers, but your garden may have alkaline soil, which precludes cultivation of these acid-loving plants. You could build raised peat beds or fill in planting holes with peat and treat the plants frequently with sulfur, but eventually the underlying soil would reassert its alkaline nature. It is much more sensible to grow the plants in suitable containers filled with a peat-enriched potting mix.

Some plants grow better in

pots than in open ground. Figs, for example, produce more fruit when grown where their roots are restricted than when they are allowed to roam. Certain rampant plants, such as mint, are also better grown in pots to keep them from overrunning the garden.

Decorating with potted plants

Even in gardens with plenty of open ground and ideal soil, there can be a need for plants in pots. A large expanse of patio, for example, can benefit from the softening effect of potted plants. A container-grown climber trained up a trellis can transform a bare house or garden wall into a vertical garden. On a more temporary note, you might want to dress up

hostas, acanthuses, and agapanthuses, grow happily and look beautiful in pots, but they die back in fall and remain dormant until spring. Unless you have an out-of-the-way spot to store them, it is better to choose evergreen perennials, such as periwinkles, bergenias, or Christmas roses, or forgo perennials altogether.

Lastly, there are many houseplants, such as palms, passionflowers, jasmines, spider plants, cacti, and succulents, that enjoy a summer stint outdoors, between the last spring frost and the first fall one. Summer showers clean the dust off their leaves, and whiteflies are less troublesome outdoors. Some flowering houseplants, such as oleanders and orange and lemon trees, benefit from exposure to summer sun; it matures the new growth, helping to encourage the production of next year's flowers.

Long-term plants
While herbaceous plants and houseplants add short-term color, woody plants add substance to a garden. Shrubs and trees in pots are doubly important if there are none in the open ground. Always try to match the size of the container to the long-term needs of the plant. You can — with bonsai-like regimes of pruning back top and root growth, restricted feeding, and watering — keep potentially huge trees and shrubs small, but it is more sensible to

▲ **Circular theme** A giant container planted with *Erysimum* 'Bowles Mauve,' a perennial with wallflower-like flowers in late spring, creates an impressive focal point, sitting like the hub of a wheel in a circle of dry-set brick paving. The circular bed at the base is filled with pansies and London pride *(Saxifraga x urbium)*, and the lines of a low, neatly trimmed box hedge emphasize the formal scale of the centerpiece.

▶ **Potted laurel** Standard-trained laurels *(Laurus nobilis)*, here clipped into pyramid shapes, are traditional subjects for container cultivation. They provide height without taking up too much ground space. The large pressure-treated wooden tubs, filled with good potting soil, are mounted on casters to facilitate moving.

▶ **Formal approach** Urns brimming with geraniums and fuchsias add color to sentinels of clipped boxwood and potted standard laurel trees.

choose plants whose mature size matches that of the container.

So many trees and shrubs are happy to grow in containers that there is no need to struggle with difficult plants. Aucubas, bays, boxwoods, camellias, citruses, euonymuses, heathers, hollies, laurustinuses, lavenders, rhododendrons, rosemaries, senecios, and skimmias are suitable broad-leaved evergreens. For deciduous shrubs, choose from ceanothuses, cotoneasters, hydrangeas, hypericums, Japanese maples, mock oranges, and ribes.

Large semimature trees can be grown in the type of planters that are often used outside public buildings, but many smaller standard trees will thrive in domestic-size tubs, such as half whiskey barrels. These are Amur maple *(Acer tataricum ginnala)*, the smaller Japanese flowering cherries, cornelian cherry *(Cornus mas)*, crab apple, mountain ash, the Kilmarnock dwarf weeping willow *(Salix caprea* 'Pendula'), and the ornamental pear *(Pyrus calleryana)*.

Standard rose "trees" in pots are a traditional summer feature, but they look so grim during the winter that compact shrub roses such as polyantha or miniature roses might be a better choice for a small garden.

Low-growing conifers, such as horizontal junipers, can be highly attractive in tubs, and there are many dwarf forms of larger conifers, including dwarf cedars and spruces. It is best to avoid fast-growing conifers, which can get leggy at the base.

For pots against walls, don't forget woody climbers: clematis, wisteria, honeysuckle, jasmine, Virginia creeper, silver-lace vine, ivy, and climbing roses. Confinement of their roots keeps these climbers relatively small, but it often encourages an exceptional production of flowers.

▶ **Cheerful informality** A cottage door is almost obscured by hanging baskets, boxes, wall pots, and tubs. Impatiens, pelargoniums, trailing fuchsias and lobelias, marigolds, and wax begonias create a riot of color.

◀ **Miniature garden** An old boot cast in concrete sprouts a miniature garden. Colorful rosettes of evergreen, succulent houseleeks *(Sempervivum)* thrive in full sun in a minimum of well-drained soil.

This may mean wrapping tubs with straw in winter to insulate the roots or frequent watering in summer. Sheltered spots are always better than exposed sites, as wind has a drying or battering effect on foliage and flowers.

Appearance Deadheading and the removal of faded flowers or damaged leaves and badly placed or broken branches keep a display looking good. Replacing spring flowers, such as pansies and forget-me-nots, with summer ones is an annual task, but from time to time you may also need to use fillers to close gaps created by plants that failed to take. Lobelia, alyssum, and sprigs of ivy are good inexpensive choices.

Use a nail brush and warm soapy water to scrub off any algae that form on pots in shade. Plants placed in partial shade — against a wall, for example — will grow toward the light and end up lopsided unless the pots are turned regularly to distribute sunlight equally.

Plant mixtures

Whether you mix plants or grow them singly in containers is entirely a matter of taste. Formally trained specimen laurels or topiary boxwoods look impressive on their own, as living sculptures. The same applies to large-scale rosette-forming plants, such as agave, dracaena, or palm. With their grand overtones, a circle of dwarf annuals around the base can look out of place; a gravel or bark mulch to conceal the soil is preferred. Standard fuchsias, however, can look beautiful with an underplanting of annuals.

Mixed planting for summer color can create a pleasantly informal effect. Some mixtures are traditional favorites: fuchsias, trailing lobelia, and petunias; and pelargoniums, silver-leaved senecio, and alyssum. When mixing bedding plants, be sure they have the same soil, feeding, watering, and light requirements. In shady spots, for example, ferns, ivies, begonias, calceolarias, Herb Robert, and impatiens all like the same conditions.

Care and maintenance

Plants growing in pots are usually more dependent on human care than those growing in the open ground, so it is important to give them the best possible start and to meet their ongoing needs.

Drainage Except for water-loving plants, such as water lilies, sweet flag, or cyperus, adequate drainage is essential. All pots need at least one good-sized drainage hole. For soil-based potting mixes, line the container with a 1 in (2.5 cm) thick layer of pebbles or broken clay flower pot pieces. (This is less important for peat-based "soilless" mixes.)

Feeding Follow the same routine as for plants grown in open ground, but never apply liquid fertilizer to dry soil. Plants grown for foliage appreciate fertilizers high in nitrates, while those grown for flowers benefit most from potash-rich fertilizers. With mixed planting, use a balanced, all-purpose fertilizer, such as

10-10-10. In pots, overfeeding is far more likely to be a problem than underfeeding, so stick to the manufacturers' recommended doses. It is even safer to use slow-release organic fertilizers.

Watering Plants dry out more quickly in pots than in the open ground. Annuals, especially, need frequent watering in hot weather, sometimes twice a day. With peat-based potting mixes, you may have to soak the whole pot in water in really dry weather. Otherwise, water runs down the inside of the pot and out through the drainage holes before the soil can absorb it. Many plants benefit from being mist-sprayed as well, in the evening or early morning.

Exposure Plants grown in pots need exactly the same light or shade as they would if grown in open ground. In addition, plants in pots are less protected from extremes of temperature, whether baking sun or freezing cold, than their field-grown counterparts.

Rock, wall, and water plants

Despite their name, rock garden plants don't need rocks at all. Just give them well-drained soil of a specific acidity or alkalinity and bright sun or dappled shade, as with any other plant. You don't have to build an elaborate rock garden in order to grow alpine plants successfully. In all but hot, humid climates, they will thrive on flat terrain. Yet because alpines are naturally low in stature, the beauty of their flowers is often lost at ground level. Use raised beds or containers to bring them nearer to eye level. Let some of the more common, less demanding types, such as aubrieta and alyssum, spill colorfully over ledges and walls, while houseleeks colonize nooks and crannies that have a minimum of soil. More difficult to grow are the high-mountain plants like the blue-trumpeted gentians. Although some do well in ordinary garden conditions, others, such as *Gentiana acaulis,* can test your gardening skills.

You can select from a wide range of beautiful rock garden plants, including perennials, miniature bulbs, and dwarf shrubs. There are mat-forming evergreens like the saxifrages that flower in winter, dwarf shrubs such as the sweet-scented daphnes, and slow-growing miniature conifers, from spreading junipers to globular cryptomerias and dome-shaped spruces.

Water — in a still pool, running stream, or cascading fountain — can add a special appeal to a garden. It contributes movement, light, and sound, as well as good conditions for true aquatics, which grow with their feet in water, and bog plants, which flourish in moisture-retentive soil. A pool of still water provides a suitable environment for plants of opposing habits with the tall, vertical lines of water irises, reeds, and rushes juxtaposed against the floating pads and beautiful cups of water lilies.

Alpine carpets An imitation rocky landscape is covered with alpines, purple polemoniums, and white columbines.

ROCK GARDEN PARTNERS

**Combine alpines with small bulbs, dwarf shrubs,
and carpet-forming plants to create
a scene of natural charm in a rock garden.**

The many delightfully flowered dwarf plants that grow naturally on mountains and on rugged terrain are collectively called alpines, or rock garden plants. Compact growth, arguably their most striking feature, is an adaption to the harsh conditions, particularly the fierce, dehydrating winds, of their natural habitat.

These small plants display a variety of interesting shapes. The neat, rounded cushions, rosettes, and mounds of thrifts, dianthuses, and certain saxifrages contrast extremely well with the jagged scenery of a rock garden. The lime-encrusted saxifrages, lewisias, and sempervivums offer distinctive rosette forms. In addition, there are vigorous carpet-forming species (aubrietas, cerastiums, and thymes) that tumble over the rocks.

The alpine category includes perennials and deciduous, evergreen, and coniferous shrubs and subshrubs (plants that are woody without developing the full woody growth of true shrubs). Many of these are popular plants that are both rewarding and undemanding to grow. Aubrieta, rock rose, and thrift, for example, flourish and flower profusely provided they are given well-drained soil and full sun.

Other rock garden plants have special requirements. They need free drainage but also require a plentiful supply of water and protection from excess moisture during winter. High-altitude alpines such as gentians, androsaces, and certain primulas are particularly demanding.

Between the two extremes is a wide range of rock garden plants that vary in habit, flowering season, flower type, and color.

Rock garden and alpine plants are rarely seen in local garden centers but may be purchased by mail from specialized nurseries. For information about suppliers, you may contact the American Rock Garden Society (P.O. Box 67, Millwood, New York 10546). A local botanical garden or horticultural society may also be of help in locating sources of rock garden plants.

Rock garden plants are usually

▼ **Spring in the rock garden** The high season for most alpine plants is mid-spring and late spring. Mats of red and purple *Aubrieta deltoidea* and gold-dust *(Aurinia saxatilis)* tumble over rock ledges, while mossy saxifrages and startling white *Arabis caucasica* 'Flore Pleno' add soft tones to the colorful scene.

▶ **Midsummer partners** Capturing the essence of a Mediterranean hillside, these alpines thrive in a sunny rock garden. The evergreen stonecrop *(Sedum reflexum)* forms a miniature forest, 8 in (20 cm) high, of bright yellow long-stalked flower heads above a ground cover of mother-of-thyme *(Thymus praecox arcticus,* syn. *T. drucei).*

The common form of thyme has rose-purple flowers and aromatic leaves, but cultivars with white, pink, lilac, or crimson blooms are also available.

◀ **Mountain avens** The evergreen, mat-forming mountain avens *(Dryas octopetala)* comes from the cold regions of northern Europe and seems inured to hardship and the stoniest, most arid soils. In early summer it covers the ground with drifts of snow-white, gold-centered flowers.

Useful as an underplanting for dwarf conifers, the mountain avens also looks spectacular flowing down a slope and backed by the glowing purple foliage of a low-growing *Berberis thunbergii* 'Atropurpurea Nana.' Here, a swath of mauve-flowered *Phlox douglasii* 'Boothman's Variety' frames the picture in front.

sold in small pots and can be planted at any time, weather permitting. During hot, dry spells, give young plants plenty of water.

Seasonal color

Since the most robust rock garden plants often flower the most freely, you get a stunning return for little effort. In creating rock garden partnerships, remember that vigorous carpet-forming species look effective planted above a ledge where they can cascade over the rock face. Try not to place them too near slower-growing tufted or mounded plants, as they will soon crowd them. The less vigorous species, however, should be intermingled to form irregular drifts. Plant the gaps between rocks with rosette-type species that will slowly spread to fill the spaces.

Creating year-round interest in a rock garden is not difficult. Dwarf conifers, which are available in prostrate, mounded, conical, and upright shapes, are a useful mainstay; evergreen foliage can be provided by the succulent green or purple rosettes of houseleeks *(Sempervivum)* and

▶ **Dwarf conifers** Slow-growing conifer spires in gold and dark green resonate with summer color from alpine pinks, aubrietas, golden alyssum, and bedding clumps of dwarf impatiens.

◀ **Easy alpines** Perennials suitable for rock gardens include blue and white violets, evergreen mounds of pink thrift *(Armeria maritima),* and cushion-forming, pink-flowered cranesbills *(Geranium dalmaticum),* which are not true alpines but are naturally dwarf and culturally compatible.

---

by the ground-hugging *Arabis ferdinandi-coburgii* 'Variegata.'

In early spring the pink-flowered cultivars of *Primula × polyantha* and blue *Hepatica nobilis* form a beautiful pairing for semi-shaded spots.

To achieve bold patches of color, grow very strong rock garden plants, like aubrieta, that have a spreading habit. The best types for spring color are *Aethionema* 'Warley Rose,' yellow alyssum *(Aurinia saxatilis),* and dwarf species and cultivated forms of phlox (such as *Phlox douglasii),* and thrift.

Before these have finished

flowering, the mossy saxifrages begin spreading a haze of dainty white, pink, or deep red flowers over mounds of neat green leaves.

A recent introduction, *Diascia* 'Ruby Fields' provides a long summer display with its unusual pink flowers. Extend the flowering season by cutting the plants back after the first bloom.

Rock roses *(Helianthemum nummularium)* also offer many attractive summer colors, from soft pinks and yellows to deep oranges and reds.

Some other summer-flowering plants to consider are *Silene schafta,* whose pink flowers continue well into fall; a lovely, spreading blue speedwell *(Veronica prostrata);* and any of the aromatic thymes (such as *Thymus praecox arcticus).* The 6 in (15 cm) high alpine asters *(Aster alpinus)* give splendid summer color with their yellow-eyed lavender or purple-blue daisy flowers. These are also pure white blooms in the cultivar 'Albus' and dark blue in 'Dark Beauty.'

For late summer, a yellow-and-blue grouping might include St.-John's-wort *(Hypericum olympicum)* and the clumpy *Campanula carpatica* with its large blue flower cups. *Gentiana septemfida* could be planted nearby to intro-

▲ **Pasqueflower** Often in bloom at Easter, the pasqueflower *(Pulsatilla vulgaris)* is a lowland plant that settles happily in well-drained soil in sunny rock gardens or raised beds. Cultivars range from white to purple, pink, and red.

▼ **Study in purple** This gold-centered purple-blue pasqueflower *(Pulsatilla vulgaris)* is joined in midspring by the lime-green bracts of euphorbias and clumps of arching blue fescue *(Festuca ovina* 'Glauca').

▲ **Harbingers of spring** In pale late-winter sunlight, the purity of simple, well-loved flowers heralds the awakening of new life. Pale lilac goblets of *Crocus tommasinianus* shimmer in a rock garden pocket, illuminating the incomparable pale yellow of the first primroses *(Primula vulgaris)* and the last drooping bells of snowdrops *(Galanthus nivalis)*.

▲ **Pools of purple** In this charming miniature rock landscape, twin peaks of compact, slow-growing junipers *(Juniperus communis* 'Compressa') rise from a sea of naturalized purplish-blue *Anemone blanda*.

▶ **Alpine carpet** Create an alpine lawn by planting a rock garden with cultivars of wild thyme *(Thymus serpyllum)*. They will knit together to form a flowering carpet throughout the summer, and provide evergreen foliage cover the rest of the year. Intermingled here are pale pink 'Annie Hall' in the foreground, white 'Album' at center, and lilac 'Lanuginosus' in back. The carpet is broken by clumps of purple *Aster alpinus*, lavender *Viola cornuta,* and pink *Geranium dalmaticum.* Silky seed heads of *Pulsatilla vulgaris* tower above the alpine "turf."

▶ **Garland flowers** Every rock garden should include a garland flower *(Daphne cneorum)*. This dwarf evergreen shrub is often temperamental, but once established, it is so glorious a plant that it amply repays the extra care. It resents root disturbance, so start with a young pot-grown specimen, which will eventually spread to several square feet. In early summer this shrub is smothered with fragrant pink flowers; the color is deeper and richer in its cultivar 'Eximia.'

The daphnes' pink swaths are enhanced by the silvery leaves of the dwarf evergreen shrub *Euryops acraeus*, which bears yellow daisy flowers in midsummer. These partners also contrast magnificently with the graceful spikes of St. Bernard's lily *(Anthericum liliago)*.

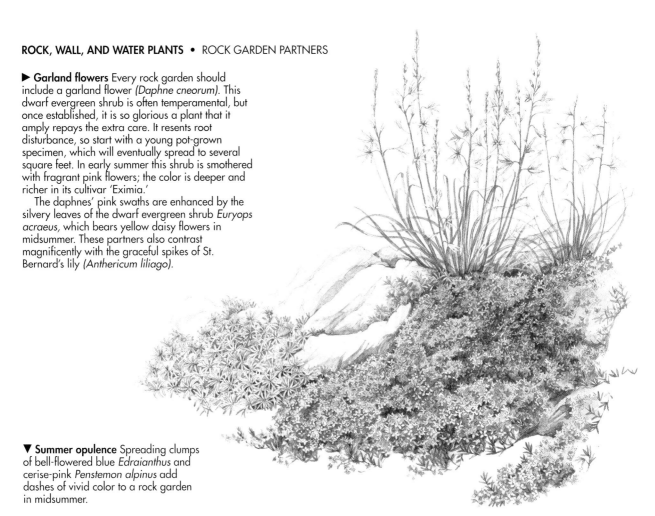

▼ **Summer opulence** Spreading clumps of bell-flowered blue *Edraianthus* and cerise-pink *Penstemon alpinus* add dashes of vivid color to a rock garden in midsummer.

to introduce a touch of intense blue. Then, in front you could add yellow-flowered *Sisyrinchium californicum brachypus.*

In early fall, *Astilbe chinensis pumila,* 1 ft (30 cm) in height, has feathery pink blooms, which are perfectly echoed by the Himalayan fleece flower *(Polygonum affine),* a plant with little rose-pink pokers. Complete the design with the silver leaves of *Artemisia schmidtiana* 'Nana.'

Choice alpines

Many distinctive rock garden plants grow in tufts or form neat clumps. Their attractive foliage is often a feature in its own right.

A lovely example is the pasque-flower *(Pulsatilla vulgaris),* so called because its flowers bloom at Eastertime. The clump of finely divided foliage appears early in spring, when downy buds open to show golden-centered mauve or purple flowers.

Some types of plants have many distinctive species or cultivars and are well worth planting in a grouping of any size. Four plants to start with are alpine pinks *(Dianthus),* true geraniums, primulas, and gentians.

The alpine pink *(Dianthus alpinus)* forms a neat, dense

mound that is hidden in summer by a generous display of single flowers whose petals have serrated edges. This species, available in a number of cultivars, looks equally lovely in a rock garden, raised bed, or as part of an alpine display in a container.

Geranium dalmaticum is one of the easiest dwarf geraniums to grow. It forms a mat of foliage covered with pink flowers in midsummer. It thrives in poor conditions, even in pavement cracks.

Primulas combine simplicity with elegance. They do best in light shade and like moist conditions and a plentiful supply of

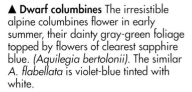

▲ **Dwarf columbines** The irresistible alpine columbines flower in early summer, their dainty gray-green foliage topped by flowers of clearest sapphire blue. *(Aquilegia bertolonii).* The similar *A. flabellata* is violet-blue tinted with white.

humus. *Primula frondosa,* as an example, responds well to a generous addition of leaf-mold to the soil, giving a spring display of golden-eyed, rose-pink flowers.

Gentians typify the beauty of alpines. Many have a reputation for being temperamental but one, *Gentiana septemfida,* produces a mass of rich blue flowers in summer without special attention. It does best in rich, moist soil.

Cracks and crevices

Alpine plants that require perfect drainage do best when grown in crevices, thus bringing life and beauty to vertical stone faces.

Stonecrops and houseleeks *(Sedum* and *Sempervivum* species) are some of the easiest plants to grow. The succulent leaves of houseleeks in particular have wonderful markings, giving a year-round display of greater value than the flowers.

The Kabschia group of saxifrages include many delightful miniatures. One of the best of these is *Saxifraga jenkinsii* with pale pink flowers in early spring. In alkaline soil the leaves of *S. jenkinsii* are often encrusted

◄ **Succulent alpines** A Mexican desert effect has been achieved by placing pots of purple-leaved echeverias and tapering agaves among hardy rock garden plants. These include carpets of variegated arabis and thyme, feathery *Artemisia schmidtiana* 'Nana,' and clumps of sempervivums and *Sedum* 'Rosea.'

◀ **Alpine tapestry** Many true rock garden plants can be mixed with dwarf perennials and spring-flowering bulbs. The plants in this flowering meadow are identified in the key above.

1 Violet *(Viola* hybrids)
2 Alpine wallflower *(Erysimum hieraciifolium)*
3 Mossy saxifrage *(Saxifraga* hybrid)
4 Aubrieta *(Aubrieta deltoidea)*
5 Gold-dust *(Aurinia saxatilis)*
6 Perennial candytuft *(Iberis sempervirens)*
7 Primrose *(Primula vulgaris)*
8 Grape hyacinth *(Muscari armeniacum)*
9 Fleabane *(Erigeron* cultivar)
10 Leopard's-bane *(Doronicum plantagineum)*
11 Daffodil *(Narcissus* cultivar)

with granules of lime, making them sparkle and glisten.

Foliage effects
It is a good idea to include some larger plants — shrubs and dwarf conifers — in the rock garden. They add height and substance, linking the smaller plants and preventing a disjointed effect. Many, such as broom *(Cytisus × kewensis),* have beautiful flowers.

The garland flower *(Daphne cneorum)* — best known for its wonderful show of scented pink blooms — has evergreen foliage, which is welcome in the winter.

The most useful kinds of conifer are the dwarf forms of false cypress *(Chamaecyparis)* and the common juniper *(Juniperus communis* 'Compressa'), which has tight upright growth.

▶ **Trumpeting gentians**
Breathtakingly blue, the high-alpine gentians are invaluable for late-spring color. The large trumpets of *Gentiana acaulis* flare next to the starlike spring gentians *(G. verna);* setting them off is a soft gray cushion of saxifrage foliage.

WALL COMMUNITIES

House walls offer a spot for pleasing color combinations, while freestanding and retaining walls welcome alpines that can almost survive without soil.

Walls offer shelter and reflected warmth and protect delicate shrubs and plants that might not otherwise withstand conditions in the North. Bare walls can be unattractive, but when covered with climbers and fronted with shrubs, flowers, and bulbs, they blend into the garden, becoming a beautiful vertical element.

Sunny south- and west-facing walls may be lifesavers for the frost-sensitive jasmine *(Jasminum officinale)* and allow its fragrant white flowers to make a romantic backdrop for a summer flower border. The many rock roses *(Cistus)* and California's "wild lilacs" *(Ceanothus* species) also appreciate such protected positions. With this bit of help, the fluffy blue flowers of *Ceanothus* look charming in late spring and early summer, especially if white-flowered *Clematis montana wilsonii* scrambles through them.

Many color schemes can be created with large-flowered clematises, such as white 'Madame le Coultre' and lavender 'W. E. Gladstone.' But they are striking amid shrubs that have flowers in contrasting shapes.

Climbing roses are good partners for clematises. Try *Clematis ×jackmanii* 'Superba' with *Rosa* 'Golden Showers' for contrast, or with the sweetly scented *R.* 'New Dawn' for harmony.

Gray- and silver-leaved plants, such as lavender, lavender cotton, and *Euphorbia characias wulfenii,* like warmth and can provide a good foil for both larger background shrubs and front plantings of, for instance, colorful South African daisies such as *Gazania, Gerbera,* and the star-shaped *Dimorphotheca.*

▶ **Stone walls** The beautiful mellow appearance of real stone walls demands restraint in embellishments. Cool green colors are in fine keeping with the gray stonework, which is complemented by the white flower heads of climbing *Hydrangea petiolaris.* Like the hostas in front, hydrangea thrives in shady, north-facing sites.

Shady walls

Garrya elliptica is one of the climbers and wall shrubs that accept shade and brighten an otherwise gloomy scene. Its festoons of lime-green catkins in late winter could be brightened by the yellow stars of *Jasminum nudiflorum.* In early summer the creamy white lace-cap blooms of the climbing *Hydrangea petiolaris* can be partnered with the scarlet flowers of the coral honeysuckle, *Lonicera sempervirens* 'Superba.'

The evergreen, climbing *Akebia quinata,* with its clusters of fragrant chocolate-purple flowers in midspring, thrives on north-facing walls. It is a handsome match for the white redbud *(Cercis canadensis),* whose white flowers open around mid May.

That splendid fruiting shrub, the oriental bittersweet *(Celastrus orbiculatus),* is another good subject for a shady wall. It doesn't need a partner, except perhaps for a green-leaved ivy as background for its rounded leaves, which turn yellow in fall. Fall is also when the

◀ **Sunny shelter** The California matilija poppy *(Romneya coulteri)* is a shrubby perennial, which should be cut back to 6 in (15 cm) stumps in fall. It flourishes best in the dry warmth of the Southwest, but survives as far north as zone 6 in the shelter of a south-facing wall. It bears scented white flowers in late summer. Ideal sun-loving companions include blue *Agapanthus* 'Headbourne Hybrids' and white-trumpeted *Crinum* x *powellii* 'Album.' Trained against the wall and framing the picture is a purple-and-white passionflower.

▲ **Wall dressing** An unattractive brick wall has become a beautiful focal point where the foliage of *Cotinus coggygria* 'Royal Purple' backs the pale pink, carmine-barred flowers of *Clematis* 'Nelly Moser.' Honeysuckle (*Lonicera periclymenum* 'Belgica') weaves its cream trumpets between them.

▼ **Old-fashioned charm** The hybrid perpetual rose 'Souvenir du Docteur Jamain' does better against a wall than in the open. It should, however, be sited out of strong sun, which can scorch the red-purple, fully double and scented blooms. It combines well with old-fashioned pale-colored pinks.

▲ **California lilacs** Away from the Pacific Coast, the magnificent wild lilacs (*Ceanothus* species) need sun and wall shelter to see them through the winter months. In spring, the rigid stems, crowded with small, glossy evergreen leaves, are almost hidden by fluffy clusters of deep blue flowers.

The blue of California lilacs is successfully set off by an underplanting of *Bellis perennis* 'Pomponette Hybrids,' with double flowers in shades of pink.

▲ **Perfection protected** Glossy, evergreen foliage and abundant, colorful double blooms make the Japanese camellias such as this cultivar, 'Pink Perfection,' most desirable shrubs. Yet even in zone 7, they may be damaged by winter cold. But in the shelter of a courtyard of a west-facing wall, they may flourish as far north as Philadelphia.

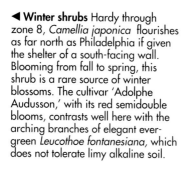

▲ **Partners for walls** The attractive evergreen coral honeysuckle *(Lonicera sempervirens)*, with its brilliant scarlet and orange flowers, is a climbing shrub that needs the support of a wall. Its complementary partner, the dainty, low-growing *Corydalis ochroleuca,* with ferny foliage and creamy flowers, is a perennial that flourishes when seeded into the cracks of a wall.

◄ **Winter shrubs** Hardy through zone 8, *Camellia japonica* flourishes as far north as Philadelphia if given the shelter of a south-facing wall. Blooming from fall to spring, this shrub is a rare source of winter blossoms. The cultivar 'Adolphe Audusson,' with its red semidouble blooms, contrasts well here with the arching branches of elegant evergreen *Leucothoe fontanesiana,* which does not tolerate limy alkaline soil.

yellow-brown fruit husks that remain from the insignificant summer flowers split open to reveal the glory of the plant — lustrous scarlet berries set within a golden lining. Be sure to use a hermaphrodite plant — one that bears both male and female flowers — otherwise it will not fruit.

Ivies, especially the variegated kinds, are useful in shade, too. The yellow-splashed leaves of *Hedera helix* 'Goldheart' contrast delightfully with the scarlet flowers of the climbing nasturtium *(Tropaeolum speciosum),* while the white and gray-green foliage of *Hedera canariensis* 'Gloire de Marengo' lightens the fall colors of Boston ivy *(Parthenocisus tricuspidata).*

Drystone walls

Retaining walls and freestanding drystone walls make excellent permanent homes for plants requiring perfect drainage — species that, in the wild, colonize steep cliffs and rocky slopes. Such plants may have a trailing, tufted, mounded, rosetted, matted, or even upright habit.

A sunny wall is ideal for the rosette-forming alpine species. In such a grouping you might include *Saxifraga cotyledon,* with its upright, delicate white and pink flowers. As a contrast to this green-leaved species, introduce dark red houseleeks such as *Sempervivum* 'Commander Hay.'

For shady walls, small ferns are a good choice. To prevent the scene from becoming too reminiscent of a dark wood, grow a flowering species such as the 3 in (7.5 cm) high pink or white fairy foxglove *(Erinus alpinus)* among the ferns.

On tall walls you can afford to grow some of the larger, upright species. For example, red valerian *(Centranthus ruber)* is an excellent choice for covering a big expanse quickly, though it may look unexciting if grown alone. By combining it with the white-tinged pink of the daisylike *Erigeron karvinskianus,* however, you can create a lovely sight.

▲ **Rocky footholds** The little *Campanula portenschlagiana* spills its cascades of violet-blue flowers in sun or shade for most of the summer. It shows itself off brilliantly against the magenta-pink of *Silene schatta.*

▼ **Drystone walls** Many easily grown rock garden plants thrive in a minimum of soil. In spring, yellow and golden *Aurinia saxatilis* and white candytuft *(Iberis sempervirens)* clothe a wall with color.

▲ **Wall footing** Small-flowered pansies *(Viola)* make excellent partners for alpines. Here, such a pansy lines the base of a retaining wall planted with pink *Geranium dalmaticum* and deep pink *Dianthus deltoides*.

▲ **Wall companions** A variety of alpines flourish in the dry soil at the base of a low, sunny wall. Tufts of pink and white thrift *(Armeria maritima)* mix their grassy foliage with the succulent leaves of variegated *Sedum kamtschaticum*. The latter sends its sprawling stems over the neat purple rosettes of the common houseleek *(Sempervivum tectorum)*.

◀ **Silvery saxifrages** Native mostly to mountain peaks, the saxifrages *(Saxifraga* species) feel at home in the crevice of a dry wall, where they form elegant rosettes of foliage. Here a specimen with silvered, lime-encrusted leaves displays in early summer a 1½ ft (45 cm) arching plume of glistening white blooms; other types bear pink, purple, or yellow blossoms. This white-flowered form seems to flow down the stones, frothing over large rosettes of *Sempervivum tectorum* and tiny whorls of a purple-tinted *Sedum*.

WATER PLANTS

Garden pools stocked with aquatics and moisture-loving wetland plants are outstanding focal points in spring and summer.

Water brings coolness, serenity, and shifting light patterns to the garden. It offers a fascinating canvas for eye-catching combinations of water- and moisture-loving plants, many of which are renowned for their exotic flowers or striking foliage.

Water lilies *(Nymphaea),* with glossy floating leaf pads and large flowers, are the mainstay of any pool. As a contrast to water lilies, try the floating water hawthorn *(Aponogeton distachyus)* with its large glossy leaves and vanilla-scented, waxy white flowers from late spring until fall. The lotuses *(Nelumbo* species) are desirable for their foliage alone — these plants hold circular leaves above the water that are as much as 3 ft (90 cm) wide. And their summertime flowers are equally spectacular, bowls of yellow, white, pink, and red that may measure 10 in (25 cm) from petal tip to petal tip.

Use marginal plants, which like to keep their feet wet, in the shallow shelf area of a pool to soften the water's edge. Try water arum *(Calla palustris),* with 1 ft (30 cm) high heart-shaped leaves and white-spathed summer flowers, in combination with forget-me-not *(Myosotis scorpiodes)* and golden club *(Orontium aquaticum),* which has metallic leaves and golden flower spikes. For dramatic vertical lines, plant reeds, rushes, and water irises, including the many types with variegated foliage.

Moisture-loving plants link the water with the rest of the garden. Among the best plant choices are feathery astilbes and meadowsweets *(Filipendula rubra* and *F. purpurea),* candelabra primulas that bear clusters of flowers in spring as well as early summer,

---

▼ **Poolside plants** The golden marsh marigold *(Caltha palustris* 'Flore Pleno') and the massive-leaved western skunk cabbage *(Lysichiton americanum),* with its showy yellow flower spadix in spring, thrive in boggy soils.

WATER PLANTS • **ROCK, WALL, AND WATER PLANTS**

◀ **Tempered wilderness** The edges of a large pool support the lush vegetation of native plants and moisture-loving perennials. Astilbes, giant cowslips *(Primula florindae),* and ostrich ferns *(Matteuccia struthiopteris)* jostle for space alongside a wooden bridge spanning the pool.

daylilies *(Hemerocallis),* rodgersias, bold clumps of hostas, ferns, and 3-5 ft (1-1.5 m) tall Japanese irises *(Iris ensata* or *I. kaempferi).*

Planning a water garden

In a formal water garden, the regular shape of the pool is all-important, and the plants become decorative features emphasizing its geometrical contours. With an informal pool, however, it is vital to blur the boundary between land and water, especially at the edge of an artificial pool.

In either case, you must choose from two distinct categories of water plants. First, there are the true water plants, which require water around their roots in order to flourish. These range from water lilies, golden clubs, and water hawthorns to wetland plants that thrive in shallow water, such as

pickerelweed, certain irises, arrowheads, marsh marigolds, and bulrushes *(Scirpus).* The so-called oxygenators such as anacharis or vallisneria, which are vital for maintaining the oxygen content of water, generally grow underwater and so play little part in the appearance of the pond.

The second category comprises moisture-loving plants that grow around the edges of a pool. They prefer moist but not waterlogged soil, in sun or light shade, and include astilbes, daylilies, hostas, Japanese and Siberian irises, gunneras, primroses, and ferns.

When deciding on water plants, consider the form, size, and leaf color as well as the flowers — exactly as you would plan groupings for herbaceous or mixed borders. The smaller the pool, the fewer varieties should be used. Select boldly contrasting leaf shapes: counter flat, round water lily leaves, for example, by the sword-like foliage of sweet flag *(Acorus calamus)* or the lacy fairy moss *(Azolla caroliniana).* Instead of creating a jumble of individual plants, group together several specimens of one carefully selected

▲ **Bog bean** The aptly named rhizomatous bog bean *(Menyanthes trifoliata)* is a useful pool plant, growing as happily in deep water as in the muddy ground that surrounds a pool. In early summer it bears clusters of pinkish-white fringed flowers that perfectly match the pink plumes of astilbes.

▼ **Marsh marigold** This poolside plant — *Caltha palustris,* also known as king cup — produces delightful clumps of heart-shaped leaves. In late spring it opens glistening buttercup flowers, whose golden rays illuminate tall red-purple Japanese primroses *(Primula japonica).*

variety, to form a distinct, natural-looking drift.

Unless you contain plants in special aquatic planting pots and baskets, choose species of roughly equal vigor; otherwise strong growers will soon swamp weaker neighbors. Try to match the vigor and potential size of a plant to the size of the pool and its surround. A gunnera, for example, can look exceedingly dramatic near water, but with a height and spread of 10 ft (3 m), it would seem out of scale with a tiny pool.

Some water plants, such as water hyacinth *(Eichhornia crassipes)* and umbrella plant *(Cyperus alternifolius),* need a cool but frost-free spot under cover to overwinter; otherwise they have to be replaced annually. And some of these plants dislike moving water, whether currents in a natural stream or the disturbance caused by an active fountain, tumbling cascade, or waterfall.

Year-round interest
A pool and its surround should be attractive in fall and winter as well as in the growing season. Though most water plants are herbaceous, some, such as sweet flag, are evergreen, and fairy moss *(Azolla caroliniana)* turns russet in fall. If moisture-loving shrubs, such as dogwood *(Cornus)* and willow *(Salix),* are planted near a pool, they can provide winter interest, especially if you choose forms with colored bark.

With good planning, you can have flowers for most of the year, either in the pool or around it. Throughout spring, marsh marigolds *(Caltha palustris)* and arrowhead *(Sagittaria* species) blossom in the pool, while primulas and globeflowers *(Trollius)* bloom around the margins. Forget-me-nots *(Myosotis scorpioides),* lotuses, and water lilies *(Nymphaea)* fill the pool with summer color; and water hawthorn *(Aponogeton distachyus)* and pickerelweed *(Pontederia cordata)* flower in fall. For fragrance, there are the aromatic leaves of sweet flag and water mint *(Mentha aquatica).* The labiate mint flowers also attract insects.

A pool and its planting should stand as a picture by itself as well as being part of the larger garden scene. Use the planting, both in and around the pool, to reinforce an existing color scheme or to

◀ **Water lilies** With their beautiful cup-shaped flowers and broad green leaf pads, water lilies *(Nymphaea)* are the most popular of all water plants. They also provide cover and shade for ornamental fish.

▶ **Foliage contrasts** Wide clumps of hostas surrounding the pool ease the transition from still water to hard pavement.

▼ **Streamside banks** Densely planted with water-loving irises and native ferns, a stream integrates naturally into the overall garden picture.

enliven it with exciting new contrasts. Most native water plants have white, yellow, or blue flowers, which make a restful combination. For a vibrant effect, use tropical and hybrid water lilies and other exotic plants in pinks, oranges, reds, or purples.

Balancing water plants

Many water plants serve useful purposes as well as being attractive. They help to create an ecological balance that is vital in still water, especially in small artificial pools without recirculating pumps. The oxygenators are the most important, but floating aquatics, marginal plants, deep water aquatics, moisture lovers, and even water lilies all play a part.

Oxygenators help to keep the water clear and "sweet." They provide oxygen for fish and other livestock, and assimilate the carbon dioxide given off by fish during respiration. They also provide fish with a place to lay their eggs. These plants keep the correct oxygen content of the water and spend all or most of their lives submerged, though some, such as *Cabomba caroliniana,* rise to the surface to flower. Many have ferny foliage, so that water can flow through them without damage.

If there is a layer of soil on the pool bottom, planting is easy. Simply tie a small weight or stone to the cut ends of a clump of oxygenators, and lower it into the water. Otherwise, plant oxygenators in a small clay flower pot filled with a heavy clay top soil mix. Some oxygenators, such as anacharis *(Elodea canadensis),* can become invasive. Take out any excess growth with a rake, and use it for compost.

Floating aquatics may be delicate, such as water clover *(Marsilea mutica),* or large-leaved, such as floating heart *(Nymphoides peltata).* Some plants, such as duckweed *(Lemna minor)* or water hyacinth *(Eichhornia crassipes),* are not anchored to the soil; they drift and reassemble in response to water currents, wind, or even the movement of fish.

Floaters provide food for fish and shade the water, which helps to curtail algae. The long, trailing roots of water hyacinth offer hiding places for fish fry and water insects. To plant, simply place them on the surface of the water.

▲ **Water meadow** In midsummer a narrow stream coursing through a meadow of grass and wild plants is edged by twin ranks of primulas. The bright golden yellow candelabra heads are borne atop 3 ft (90 cm) tall stems rising from shiny evergreen leaf rosettes.

▲ **Moisture lovers** By late spring, the bog primula *(Primula florindae)* is in full, scented bloom, raising its heads of cowsliplike yellow bells on white-dusted stems up to 3 ft (90 cm) tall. The yellow theme continues with glossy-leaved monkey flower *(Mimulus luteus)*, partnered by elegant blue Jacob's ladder *(Polemonium caeruleum)*.

▼ **Summer by the pool** Sheltered by sword-shaped, variegated iris foliage, Algerian marsh orchids *(Dactylorrhiza elata)* push up their dense spikes of purple blossoms in early summer. The color is repeated nearby in the purple-pink flowers of *Primula japonica,* nodding above the large heart-shaped leaves of *Caltha palustris*.

▲ Pool planting The clean lines of a formal pool should never be obscured. Highlight its geometric shape with one or two corner clumps of shallow-water sweet flags or irises, and let water lilies occupy much of the center.

Some, such as fairy moss and duckweed, form winter buds or turons, which sink to the bottom of the pool in fall and rise again the following spring.

Water lilies, with their exotic flowers, are popular water plants. Their leaves serve a practical purpose, sheltering fish, shading the water, and preventing the growth of unwanted algae.

Hundreds of cultivars are available. Most are hardy and flower during daylight hours. In leaf and flower size they range from miniatures to giants with blooms and leaf pads as large as dinner plates. Hardy water lilies vary in color from pure white to pink, red, yellow, orange, and copper, many changing to darker shades on successive days. Tender or tropical water lilies are also available that can be planted in early summer in shallow water that is at least 70°F (21°C), or in indoor heated pools; some bloom at night; their showy flowers, often with crimped or frilled edges, are exotic colors, including blue and purple.

Some water lilies require water up to 3 ft (90 cm) deep, while others will flourish in shallow pools and even tubs with a surface area of 2 sq ft (60 sq cm). Make sure you choose a type that matches the depth and space available. A pool entirely covered with rampant water lily pads is ecologically unsound as well as unattractive. (As a rule, only 60 to 70 percent of the water surface should be covered by plants.)

In natural ponds, water lilies can be lowered into the water with their roots placed between two squares of turf, but they are easier to control if you plant them in submerged plastic tubs.

Deep-water aquatics are good alternatives to water lilies, and are planted in much the same way. They include the lotuses (*Nelumbo* species), which flourish in water 3-4 ft (90-120 cm) deep, and the white water hawthorn (*Aponogeton distachyus*), with its long flowering period and attractive boat-shaped leaves.

Marginals or wetland plants are by far the largest category. Some examples are sweet flag, marsh marigold, and forget-me-not. They need either shallow water or continually moist soil, although some are happy in both. Marginals are not as essential to the ecology as oxygenators, although the mini jungle created by their roots and stems offers good hiding places for young fish. Like other water plants, they absorb minerals from the water and thus suppress algae.

Poolside plants

This large category covers a range of species, from those that qualify as marginals to ordinary border plants — such as hostas, astilbes, and globeflowers — that like, but don't require, moisture at the roots. Most true bog plants prefer damp rather than wet soil.

In artificial pools the water is held in a liner or concrete shell, so the adjacent soil may be bone-dry. To create a bog-garden effect with a smooth, gradual transition between water and land, choose such moisture lovers as *Iris sibirica*, hostas, or primulas.

◀ **Waterside companions** The orange-red daisylike flowers of *Ligularia dentata* 'Desdemona' instantly catch the eye, and the lustrous deep green leaves backed with bright purple are equally spectacular. This moisture-loving perennial demands bold partners, such as large-leaved western skunk cabbage *(Lysichiton americanum)* and royal fern *(Osmunda regalis).*

▶ **Marginal plants** Where a rock garden slopes down to an informal pool, moist pockets of soil form that are ideal for the incomparable hostas. Magnificent in their diverse leaf shapes and colors, from bluish green to lime-yellow, they fit naturally into pool plantings. Their rounded forms are contrasted by upright purple *Iris laevigata.*

▼ **Cotton grass** Ideal for shallow water and bog gardens, the elegant cotton grass *(Eriophorum latifolium)* makes an unusual partner for the golden-flowered marsh marigold *(Caltha palustris).* The cotton-wool tufts of white flowers introduce a cool element to the pool's lily pads and, on the far side, the vertical clumps of sweet flag *(Acorus calamus).*

▲ **Miniature pools** Waterproof tubs and barrels make excellent "pools" for a patio. They can be planted with small water lilies and, as here, with the unusual nonflowering water horsetail *(Equisetum)*.

◄ **Water hawthorn** In addition to its distinctively long floating leaves, the water hawthorn *(Aponogeton distachyus)* bears clusters of sweetly scented, pure white flowers in summer.

▼ **Informal pools** Small pools need careful planting. Introduce deep and shallow-water plants that don't crowd the surface. Light and air are crucial to maintaining an ecological balance.

MOVING WATER

**The sound and sight of moving water brings life
and sparkle to a garden — and even the smallest space
can boast a delightful water feature.**

Moving water is an unending source of attraction; its appearance constantly changes according to the light, the weather, and its surroundings. Water pleases the eye and the ear and evokes dreamy, peaceful feelings.

In a large garden the sound of moving water stirs interest long before the source itself is visible. In a smaller garden moving water is automatically a focal point.

In practical terms, the movement adds oxygen to the water, so any fish benefit. The spray from a fountain also helps cleanse the water's surface by sinking dust.

Few gardens are blessed with natural moving water, but it is easy to install a fountain or watercourse. Many features come in kits. If you are handy, you can also combine different fixtures into a unique design.

Waterfalls and cascades involve water dropping from higher to lower levels. A waterfall is a continuous drop, while a cascade is a series of some smaller, connected waterfalls or steep channels, often with pools in between. You can buy preformed waterfalls or cascades in rigid plastic or molded fiberglass, or you can use flexible liners to build a watercourse.

Fountains are jets of spouting or bubbling water; they can be freestanding or mounted on a garden wall.

Custom-built water features
You can make your own fountain by connecting a water supply to any weatherproof, waterproof container, such as an urn, old copper washbasin, stone sink, or half barrel. Artificial streams can be constructed from natural stone or waterproofed concrete.

On a larger scale, such projects are best undertaken with professional advisers and contractors. If

▶ **Natural streams** Moisture-loving marginals emphasize the winding course of a natural stream. Swaths of golden monkey flowers *(Mimulus luteus)* catch the bright light and are reflected in the water.

▲ Animal-shaped fountain Fish, herons, swans, dolphins, seals, and frogs are popular as water fountains. They can be mounted on stone or concrete display pedestals to make them more visible and thus increase their impact.

▼ Contemporary style A group of polished stainless-steel mushroom sprays of differing heights creates an impressive focal point. Tall fountains should be sited so that strong winds won't blow the water off course.

▲ Traditional feature Available in a variety of different guises, standard pool fountains usually represent mythological creatures or classical figures. Here, a boy bears a scalloped bowl, a popular choice for a more formal setting.

Pool fountains can be made of stone, concrete, lead, bronze, copper, terra-cotta, plastic, or fiberglass, and vary in price depending on the material, size, and style.

Fountains installed in pools that contain water lilies and ornamental fish should be restricted to a small, softly playing jet of water.

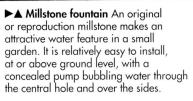

▶▲ **Millstone fountain** An original or reproduction millstone makes an attractive water feature in a small garden. It is relatively easy to install, at or above ground level, with a concealed pump bubbling water through the central hole and over the sides.

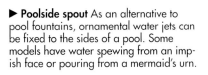

▶ **Poolside spout** As an alternative to pool fountains, ornamental water jets can be fixed to the sides of a pool. Some models have water spewing from an impish face or pouring from a mermaid's urn.

▲ **Miniature waterfall** Water recirculated from a pump in a raised pool trickles through a pipe into a narrow watercourse on a lower level.

If you are adding a fountain, waterfall, or cascade to an existing pool, the location is relatively fixed. If starting from scratch, try to site the water feature where it will get some sun, since moving water is most attractive when it catches the light.

You need a nearby electrical outlet to run the pump. Make sure that the receptacle has a ground fault interrupter and that the cable is adequately protected. Consult an electrician to make sure you meet local codes.

Site a fountain in a sheltered spot, where strong winds won't blow the spray off course. For the same reason, don't place it too close to a path.

Waterfalls and cascades
A small waterfall or cascade can still be effective — even a drop of 6 in (15 cm) is enough. The smaller the amount of water circulating, though, the narrower the waterfall head should be to get the maximum effect. Many designs have center-pouring "lips" for small flows of water.

Preformed molds of rigid plastic or more expensive fiberglass are quick and easy to install. They can look quite natural, but you are limited to the shapes, sizes, and colors available.

You can also use sheets of flexible waterproof liners for watercourses. Made of polyethylene, butyl, or specially reinforced PVC, these come in a range of sizes — if necessary, two liners can be joined together with special waterproof tape or by vulcanizing. Life expectancies range from 5 to 50 years, with prices and guarantees to match.

Liners are more difficult to install than preformed molds. To prevent punctures, place the liner on a 1 in (2.5 cm) layer of clean sand that is covered with a special matting. Design opportunities are wider with a liner, and if the edges are concealed, a more natural-looking result is possible.

Concrete watercourses are rarely made nowadays, because of the cost, the skilled labor needed, and the risk of cracking with age or from frost. However, a concrete "stone" ledge with water spilling over it is an attractive possibility.

Pool fountains
The simplest fountains consist of a jet installed in a pool. The spray

any natural water is diverted, the approval of local environmental boards and planning authorities may be needed.

Design decisions
Water features and the mechanical equipment needed to operate them can be quite expensive, so cost is a prime concern — although other factors play a part.

In small gardens, small-scale water features are best. A wall-mounted fountain or a self-contained patio fountain is suitable. Be sure to buy good-quality fixtures, since they will all be viewed at close range. In larger gardens, size depends on location. A fountain in the middle of a lawn should be large enough to command attention.

Waterfalls and cascades need slopes or vertical level changes.

Few gardens have these naturally, but a common solution for level gardens is to use the soil dug out during the construction of a pool to build an adjacent rock garden, down which water can fall.

A fountain looks best in a formal pool, while a waterfall or cascade is usually better with a natural-looking pool. A waterfall connecting formal pools on two levels can be successful, provided it does not pretend to be natural; formal, steplike cascades are another option.

Neither fish nor water lilies survive long in a small pool with a vigorous fountain, although a single small jet, used occasionally, does no harm.

Watercourses made from concrete or systems of vinyl or rubber liners look more natural if they are kept fairly narrow and winding. The natural effect can be enhanced by covering the base of the course with dark gravel or rounded pebbles and placing some larger stones here and there to create ripples in the water.

is usually created by a submersible pump, whose power determines the height that the spray will reach.

Spray heads may be made of polished stainless steel, brass, terra-cotta, and plastic. Most single jets have only one spray pattern, such as a geyser, plume, or revolving arc. A "water bell" jet has a bell-shaped spray; single and multiple types are available.

Some jets have interchangeable heads, each one producing a different spray pattern. Others provide a repeating series of spray patterns, with several changes per minute. There are also jets that mix air with water to produce a foaming plume.

Some jets have an optical lighting system, which illuminates a fountain from below. As a rule, single-color systems are the most

◄ **Imitating nature** A large rock garden incorporates a waterfall flowing over flat stones. The edges of the watercourse are lushly planted with moisture-loving hostas, ferns, and astilbes, and tall, purple-flowered *Iris sibirica*.

▼ **Split-level pools** Three interconnected raised pools create a fascinating water feature. A fountain in the center pool adds sound and movement without disturbing the fish in the upper pool.

▲ Small-scale water features Any frostproof container large enough to contain a pump can be made into an attractive water feature. Here, a terra-cotta urn softly spilling water adds a Mediterranean touch to the brick surround of a raised pool.

▶ Oriental water spout The introduction of a simple water feature turns a secluded corner of a garden into a haven of peace and tranquillity. A bamboo water spout lets water trickle into a miniature basin set between rocks.

restful, and white lights are the most natural.

Traditional pool fountains often represent mythological creatures or classical figures. Fauns, cherubs, nymphs, or sea gods, all make a garden seem more formal.

Animal-shaped pool fountains come in the form of herons, swans, dolphins, frogs, seals, and fish. Simple and ornate basins, scallop shells, and bowls shaped like flowers or overlapping lotus leaves are available fitted with jets. Some manufacturers offer optional pedestals to increase height and visual impact.

Self-contained fountains

If you don't have a pool, but would still like a fountain, opt for a self-contained unit that has a collection basin either at the top — much like a drinking fountain or bird bath — or at the base. It needs very little water and only a small pump, so you can put it in almost any place where the sound of water would be soothing.

Designs can be simple to ornate, and range from the modern to the classical. Some statues and bowls can be bought separately, thus giving a wider choice. Test your choice to be sure that its tubing will deliver a proper flow of water and its basin will hold enough water to keep the fountain working continuously.

Wall and bubble fountains

Inspired by natural springs, bubble fountains usually have a round, flat stone from which a gentle, central flow of water emerges. The even film of water trickling over the stone surface enhances its beauty.

Original millstones are costly and hard to find, but a good substitute may be cast in Portland cement, or fashioned from a naturally flat rock. Such a stone is set over a shallow water tank and plastic sheeting, which collects the water. The stone can be displayed at ground level, or higher, depending on whether the water tank is buried. The plastic sheeting can be covered with a layer of smooth, dark pebbles.

Wall fountains save space. Dolphins, lion masks, and gargoyles are usually set in plaques for easy mounting and have a collection basin underneath. The basin can be simple or ornate, and large or small, depending on available space and the flow of the water. A wall fountain can also be set to empty directly into a pool.

Scented partners

Fragrance is elusive and intangible — and it can be delicate or cloying. We instinctively turn to flowers of exquisite shape and color for scent, but are often disappointed. In their quest for perfect hue and form, plant breeders have largely sacrificed fragrance. So, in order to recapture a perfumed garden, we often have to revert to old-fashioned flower species.

Many blooms have unforgettable scents — the sweet fragrance of jonquil narcissi, the heady smell of lilacs after rain, the spicy aroma of old-fashioned roses and certain lilies, and the unexpected, almost overpowering redolence of *Chimonanthus praecox* in midwinter. In summer, garden perfumes are most noticeable on warm evenings, when the essential flower oils are released into the air.

As each scent tends to be distinctive, it is best not to mix them. Delicate rose fragrances should not have to compete with strongly redolent honeysuckles, nor sweet lavender with clove-scented pinks.

Aromatic foliage, notably that of herbs, is less overt than flower perfumes and usually has to be bruised or pinched to release its scent. Savory rosemary or bay is perfect for planting around a barbecue pit, unlike the pungent rue and the aniseed-scented fennel, whose odors always linger in their immediate surroundings.

Perfumed plants should ideally be grown where they can be readily encountered. Place scented climbers and wall shrubs near house windows and doors, or train them on pillars and arbors near a patio. Grow fragrant nicotianas, wallflowers, and old-fashioned pinks close to a path, hyacinths and scented stocks in window boxes, and verbenas in hanging baskets.

Fragrant roses 'George Arend's ' strong perfume complements the visual beauty of climber 'American Pillar.'

FRAGRANT ROSES

**Loved for its perfect form, pure colors,
and exquisite fragrance, the majestic rose
has endured for thousands of years.**

It is often said that modern roses have little or no fragrance. It is true that plant breeders, in their quest for perfect form, clear color, and continual bloom, have often produced roses whose scent is at best elusive. However, many of the modern roses — bushes, shrubs, and climbers — stand out as much for their fragrance as for their flower shape and color.

Position scented roses where their fragrance can waft across the garden or through open windows. Ideally, you should place them in a sunny spot that also receives light shade during the hottest hours of the day. In bright sun, the wine-red 'Souvenir du Docteur Jamain,' for example, may suffer sun scorch and lose some of its strong fragrance.

Modern bush roses

The large-flowered bush roses, better known as hybrid teas, are possibly the best loved of all roses. They are popular for their shapely double-flowered blooms on sturdy stems and for their long flowering season. They are perfect as cut flowers, especially those with exquisite fragrance, such as the dark red 'Chrysler Imperial,' the red-and-white 'Double Delight' with its spicy perfume, and the yellow-orange 'Sutter's Gold.' One of the most strongly scented and the longest lasting as a cut flower is the bright red 'Dolly Parton,' which is an unusually disease-resistant cultivar, as is the aptly named coral-colored 'Fragrant Cloud.' For redolent whites, few can match the large-flowered bush rose 'White Lightning.'

Cluster-flowered bush roses, or floribundas, differ little from the large-flowered roses, except that the single, semidouble, or double flowers are borne in large clusters on more branching and vigorous bushes. Scented cultivars include the yellow, coral, and red 'Circus'; the pure white 'Iceberg'; 'Ivory Fashion,' with its buttered centers; and the intensely fragrant, pink 'Angel Face.' The free-flowering 'Dusky Maiden' offers aromatic, deep crimson blooms,

---

▼ **Bed of roses** The scent of climbing and rambling roses rises high above pink and dusky red modern bush roses. Sweet-smelling lavender is a traditional partner to roses, in the garden and in potpourris.

while 'Betty Prior' produces fine five-petaled pink blossoms that resemble the perfumed sprays of flowering dogwood.

Shrub and climbing roses

Like the old roses, from which they have been bred, shrub roses are less formal in habit than bush roses. They belong in shrub and mixed borders or serve as specimen plants. They may bear their flowers singly or in small clusters. Though some modern shrubs flower repeatedly through summer to fall, many preserve the old roses' pattern of blooming just once (though abundantly) in early summer. Useful as landscaping plants, the fragrant shrub roses look perfect near sitting areas. Choose between that old favorite, the pink 'Constance Spry' with a heavy scent of myrrh, and the deeply fragrant apricot 'Alchymist,' the yellow 'Maigold,' or 'Lavender Lassie.'

The "new" English shrub roses combine the color range and repeat-flowering behavior of modern shrub roses with the form and heady fragrance of old roses.

The repeat-flowering modern climbers include several fragrant cultivars. They are ideal for training over pergolas and arbors or up pillars; let the more vigorous types climb up tall house walls and trees. The following are notable for their scent: 'City of York' (white), 'Compassion' (salmon-pink and orange), 'Don Juan' (crimson), 'Golden Showers' (yellow), and 'New Dawn' (pale pink).

Old roses

In the fifth century B.C. Herodotus, the Greek "father of history," described a rose with 60 petals whose scent was more overpowering than any other. Scholars speculate that he meant *Rosa damascena*, whose richly perfumed blossoms have been used to make rose water —"attar" of roses — since ancient times. Oil distilled from its petals was used in the commercial production of

◀ **Modern scents** Bush roses, better known as floribundas and hybrid teas, are exquisite in form though less fragrant than their ancestors. Some, however, such as 'Fragrant Cloud' *(background)*, are heavily scented, especially in fall. The scarlet 'Lilli Marlene' *(foreground)* and the vigorous, clear pink 'Queen Elizabeth' have a more delicate scent.

perfumes and rose water. (The ancient Chinese also cultivated roses on a massive scale, including the highly fragrant varieties. These flowers were also used for distilling rose oil and water, although such luxuries were reserved for the nobility.)

Many of the old roses deserve a place in the modern garden. The best are exquisitely formed, and nearly all are strongly fragrant. Although most flower heavily only once in the season, generally in early summer, many repeat sparingly, bearing the occasional flower through to fall.

Species roses are the wild ancestors of modern roses. Chiefly distinctive for their foliage, strong prickles, and outstanding hips, many work well as specimen shrubs. The sweetbrier (*Rosa rubiginosa*, syn. *R. eglanteria),* a wild rambler from Europe, offers a particularly unusual scent: the applelike perfume that fills warm summer evenings comes not from the flowers but from glands on the foliage. The Scotch rose (*R. pimpinellifolia)* is a suckering, thorny shrub with richly scented, though small, pale pink, white, or yellow blooms.

Species roses produced a number of hybrids and sports (spontaneous mutations that change one branch of a shrub), either naturally or by crossbreeding, and these so-called old-fashioned roses were widely grown until the hybrid teas were introduced in the 19th century. Many were heavily scented; several have survived to perfume modern gardens.

Alba roses are strong-growing shrubs, 6 ft (1.8 m) or more tall, with finely toothed leaves and a mass of large, pale-colored flowers, sweetly scented and often quartered in shape. Among the best and most readily available are 'Celestial' ('Céleste'), with soft pink semidouble blooms; the more fragrant 'Great Maiden's Blush,' a survivor from the 15th century with full-petaled, blush-pink flowers; and 'Königin von Dänemark,' with quartered pale pink blooms.

Bourbon roses are crosses between damask and China roses that have inherited the intense fragrance of the former and the repeat-flowering habit of the latter. The huge, full-petaled and quartered flowers are borne on spreading shrubs about 6 ft

(1.8 m) tall, with a profusion of deliciously scented flowers, purple-pink in 'Mme. Isaac Pereire' and white- and crimson-budded in 'Boule de Neige.'

Cabbage roses, also known as Provence roses, are derived from *Rosa centifolia,* and although more compact in habit (up to 6 ft/1.8 m tall), they need support for the floppy, thorny stems. Clusters of deeply fragrant, double and flat-topped flowers appear in midsummer. Two good examples are 'Fantin-Latour,' pale pink shaded with deeper blushes, and 'Rose de Meaux,' a dwarf shrub with small, bright pink blooms.

Damask roses are the most fragrant of all. Their double flowers, 3 in (7.5 cm) wide and often with incurved centers, are shaded from dark pink to white. They are held in loose clusters in early and midsummer and are followed by slender and hairy hips. Outstanding cultivars include gray-leaved and pink-flowered 'Celsiana'; the darker pink, richly scented 'Gloire de Guilan'; and the pure white, green-eyed 'Mme. Hardy.'

Gallica roses are the oldest and largest group of the old roses. They thrive in poor soil but will not tolerate shade. They grow 4-5 ft (1.2-1.5 m) high, with richly scented double flowers in midsummer. 'Belle de Crécy' is of lax habit and may need support for its thornless stems carrying purple-red flowers that mature to violet. 'Rosa Mundi,' the old and well-known striped rose ('Versicolor'), is conspicuously red and white, while 'Tuscany Superb' is notable for its velvety, golden-centered purple blooms.

Hybrid musk roses are bushy and spreading and known for their small, deliciously scented flowers borne in large clusters from late summer until the fall frosts. The apricot-yellow 'Buff Beauty' with a tealike fragrance is one of the finest; 'Penelope,' 5 ft (1.5 m) tall, has broad glossy foliage and musk-scented blooms of flushed apricot, fading to pale yellow.

Moss roses were the mainstay of Victorian rose gardens and much loved for their deeply fragrant summer blooms. They are characterized by resin-scented mossy glands on the sepals and by bristly stems. 'Nuits de Young' bears small velvety flowers of deep maroon-purple with prominent golden centers. 'William Lobb,' an ideal pillar rose, is crimson fading to lavender.

Rugosa roses are among the most popular of the old roses and widely used for hedging and as specimen shrubs. They are ultra-hardy (often to zone 2) and vigorous, with prickly stems and wrinkled leaves that turn yellow in fall among large orange-red hips. The single or double flowers appear mainly in midsummer but continue sporadically until early fall. The large bowl-shaped flowers are heavily scented.

Popular, readily available cultivars include the double-flowered yellow 'Agnes,' the magnificent white 'Blanc Double de Coubert,' and the pale pink 'Fru Dagmar Hastrup.' The double-flowered crimson 'Roseraie de l'Hay' has a scent like sugared almonds and blooms almost continuously.

▼ **Arctic sea** The glistening white, rounded forms of 'Iceberg' roses rise from unruffled waves of fragrant lavender. The swell of mixed purple lavenders — the darker-colored, compact form near the front is *Lavandula angustifolia* 'Hidcote' — washes forward into a white foam of snow-in-summer (*Cerastium tomentosum*).

PERFUMED PLANTS

**From sunny and sheltered corners of beds
and borders, or other garden spots, scented flowers
and aromatic foliage delight our senses.**

Many flowers have evolved bold colors, special shapes, and tasty nectar to attract pollinating insects; some have also developed scents for the same reason.

Leaves, too, can be aromatic — particularly those of herbs and shrubs from the Mediterranean or areas with a similar climate. The scent comes from the release of volatile oils, which evolved to reduce water loss and to deter grazing animals. Sometimes, however, the smell is not apparent until the leaves are pinched, bruised, or even crushed.

The biggest and brightest flowers are not always the most fragrant — in fact, it is often the smaller, even insignificant, flowers that smell most strongly. In addition, many highly cultivated plants, such as modern roses, carnations, and sweet peas, have lost the fragrance they once had in their primitive forms.

Generally, scents are stronger on hot, sunny days than on cold, overcast ones — this is particularly true of shrubs with aromatic leaves, which release their oils in such conditions. Even winter-scented flowers are more fragrant during milder spells. Roses, honeysuckles, jasmine, lilacs, and stocks smell best after rain.

Because fragrant plants include annuals, biennials, perennials, bulbs, shrubs, or climbers, you can place sweet-smelling plants almost anywhere in the garden — on a patio or near a door or window, for instance.

Patio plants

The gaps between the paving stones of a patio make an ideal site for a small group of plants whose leaves must be crushed to release their scent. These plants can be gently walked upon, but will not stand up to constant trampling.

Many small perennials are also suitable for patios. The dense, mat-forming cultivars of thyme *(Thymus serpyllum)* need full sun and revel in the warmth reflected from stone. In spring and summer, the prostrate Corsican mint *(Mentha requienii)* is studded with tiny lavender-colored flowers, and its leaves smell strongly of peppermint. Blooming later and larger in size, pennyroyal *(Mentha pulegium)* is extremely minty. Variegated apple mint *(Mentha suaveolens* 'Variegata') is also pleasantly minty. The common chamomile *(Chamaemelum nobile),* in its nonflowering form 'Treneague,' is a fragrant grass substitute. Yellow stonecrop *(Sedum acre)* spreads rapidly, while thrift forms neat, small mounds.

Container plants

A container of fragrant plants can

▼ **Lilac season** Late spring and early summer arrive with the heady fragrance of lilac *(Syringa)*. The dense, upright panicles range in color from white and yellow to blue, red, and purple.

perfumed climber is white-flow-ered summer jasmine *(Jasminum officinale),* which, like honey-suckle, smells much stronger dur-ing the evening.

Climbing roses enhance any doorway. Some fragrant examples include the velvety 'Climbing Crimson Glory,' yellow 'Rêve d'Or,' and cerise-pink 'Zéphirine Drouhin.' Other suitable climb-ers include the sweet autumn clematis *(Clematis paniculata),* and the plume clematis *(C. flam-mula),* both of which bloom in the fall, bearing strongly fragrant lit-tle flowers. One of the southern favorites is the Carolina jes-samine *(Gelsemium sempervir-ens),* which is hardy to zone 7 and bears its perfumed yellow flowers in midspring.

▲ **Sweet scent** The Chinese *Osmanthus delavayi* is a slow-growing, frost-sensitive evergreen with sweetly scented white flowers in midspring. It flourishes in sun or light shade. *O. heterophyllus* is similar, but somewhat hardier.

▼ **Fragrant woodbine** The common honeysuckle or woodbine *(Lonicera periclymenum)* bears clusters of redolent creamy white and red blooms. Flowering from early summer on, it thrives on walls of any exposure.

brighten up and perfume any cor-ner of the garden — from a box under a window to a pot on a pa-tio. One advantage is that you can move a container to wherever the scent can best be appreciated.

Suitable plants for containers include wallflowers, sweet Wil-liams, primroses, polyanthuses, and, later in the year, petunias, Virginia and night-scented stocks, mignonettes, and nicotianas. Hy-acinths are also fragrant, as are some of the lilies, such as *Lilium regale, L. speciosum, L. auratum,* and *L. formosanum.*

A tub of blooming pelargoni-ums has a distinctive smell, espe-cially after watering. Surround this with pots of scented-leaf pelargoniums, which have unim-pressive flowers but attractively shaped and often variegated fo-liage that releases strong scents when pinched. *Pelargonium crisp-um* 'Prince Rupert Variegated,' for example, has a lemon scent; others smell of peppermint, orange, chocolate, nutmeg, or apples.

Framing doors and windows
Door and window frames are per-fect places for training fragrant climbing plants, so that their scents are wafted into the house or enjoyed as you step out.

Sweetly scented climbers such as the honeysuckles spring to mind although, surprisingly, not all honeysuckles are fragrant. *Lonicera periclymenum* and the evergreen *L. japonica* 'Halliana' are scented.

Another old-fashioned sweetly

▲ **Perfumed wall companions** Time and patience are amply rewarded with a magnificent late-spring pairing of *Wisteria sinensis* and *Rosa banksiae lutea*. On a vast sunny wall, pale mauve, vanilla-scented wisteria tassels mingle with the near-evergreen yellow rose, whose delicately fragrant blooms resemble double primroses.

▶ **Evening scent** The sweet-smelling flowering tobacco *(Nicotiana)* blooms unceasingly throughout summer. Most modern cultivars open their flowers during the day, but the scent is most powerful at night, especially in the white-flowered form 'Fragrant Cloud.'

◀ **Night-scented stock** All stocks are fragrant, but the night-scented stock *(Matthiola longipetala bicornis)*, a hardy annual, has a more intoxicating sweetness than any other. In late summer the heady perfumes of white-flowered nicotianas and delicate pink-flowered night stock scent the evening air. Clumps of white sweet William *(Dianthus barbatus)* and red-tinged mignonettes *(Reseda odorata)* provide strong daytime fragrances.

▶ **Scent of roses** The large-flowered hybrid tea rose 'Irish Gold' is a sturdy, dark-leaved rose with an abundance of yellow flowers in summer and fall. Their light fragrance is augmented by strongly perfumed flowering tobacco *(Nicotiana alata* 'Lime Green'), which contrasts vividly with purple-leaved *Berberis thunbergii* 'Atropurpurea.'

▲ **Flowering hedge** The Persian lilac *(Syringa* x *persica* 'Alba') forms a rounded shrub smothered in late spring with panicles of scented white flowers. Their spicy perfume almost overwhelms the fragrance of the accompanying pink-and-lilac broom *(Cytisus scoparius* 'Zeelandia').

◀ **Mock orange** The rich orangelike fragrance of *Philadelphus microphyllus* fills the air around an early-summer composition in white. The small-leaved branches of mock orange, festooned with white flowers, arch down to greet the white blossoms of an evergreen *Escallonia* and the bell-shaped flowers of *Campanula alliariifolia.*

Edging plants

Plant aromatic-leaved plants alongside a sunny path to be brushed against as you pass. The fragrances released by lavender, rosemary, lavender cotton, southernwood *(Artemisia abrotanum)*, and rue, particularly on a hot day, are reminiscent of the scented scrublands of the Mediterranean.

If the path travels along the base of a retaining wall, take the opportunity to grow some scented plants along the top of it. Suitable varieties include catmint, sweet alyssum, pinks, golden-leaved marjoram, and the larger kinds of thyme, such as *Thymus* × *citriodorus* and *T. vulgaris*.

Border plants

One of the few scented plants among "standard" perennials is *Phlox paniculata* — its white and mauve cultivars are the best. Bergamot *(Monarda didyma)* has red, pink, or purple hooded flowers in whorls; the whole plant is aromatic, as is the burning bush *(Dictamnus albus)*.

In late spring, sweetly scented lilies of the valley *(Convallaria majalis)* bloom, followed by lupines, pinks, and garden carnations. In midsummer, exotic lilies mingle with roses and later with fragrant chrysanthemums.

Scented annuals and bedding plants such as wallflowers, sweet Williams, and primroses can be used in borders with sweet peas, perhaps trained along a fence, for summer fragrance. You can also choose mignonettes *(Reseda odorata);* the various stocks with clovelike scents; cherry-pie *(Heliotropium arborescens)*, whose common name describes its scent; and the hybrid verbenas, though the red ones are scentless.

Spring and summer scents

Daphnes are exquisitely scented shrubs. *Daphne mezereum* has purple-pink flowers on its leafless branches from late winter on. The dwarf evergreen garland flower *(D. cneorum)* and the spicy-scented *D.* × *burkwoodii*, both rose-pink, follow in late spring and early summer.

Azara microphylla, a small evergreen tree with yellow vanilla-scented flowers, provides one of the first smells of spring. Also evergreen, *Osmanthus heterophyllus* has profuse white, almost jasminelike flowers in fall. The

▲ **Honey-scented azalea** The deciduous azalea *(Rhododendron luteum)* bears large clusters of fragrant yellow trumpets in midspring to late spring. As a bonus, the leaves take on orange, scarlet, and purple tints in fall.

▶ **Summer scents** On hot, still summer days the combined fragrances of mock orange *(Philadelphus)* and cottage-garden lavender are reminiscent of scented Mediterranean scrublands.

▼ **Thyme cover** The mat-forming species of thyme *(Thymus serpyllum)* makes a delightfully fragrant carpet. These plants will creep over rock gardens and raised beds, and among paving cracks, releasing a strong aroma from their leaves. The flowers are also scented.

▲ **Window frames** The sweet-scented climbing rose 'Zéphirine Drouhin' is perfect for framing windows and doors. Its cerise-pink semidouble flowers are particularly fragrant in fall.

▼ **Sweet mignonette** This hardy annual *(Reseda odorata)* is a popular cottage-garden plant, prized by bees for its yellow, white, and orange flower heads, tinged red in some cultivars.

yellow azalea *(Rhododendron luteum)* is extremely fragrant.

Lilacs, which begin to bloom in late spring, have a heady fragrance and come in many colors. The white summer flowers of mock orange *(Philadelphus)* fill the air with their pervasive scent.

For late summer fragrance, very good choices are honey-scented *Buddleia davidii* and two members of the pea family with panicles of golden yellow flowers, the Mount Etna broom *(Genista aethnensis)* and the Spanish broom *(Spartium junceum)*.

Winter scents

Many winter-flowering plants carry perfumes, a high percentage of them being shrubs. Plant them near a path where they can be easily enjoyed.

Among the deciduous shrubs that bear flowers uncluttered by leaves is the Chinese witch hazel *(Hamamelis mollis)*. Its penetrating scent comes from clusters of yellow spiderlike flowers in late winter into early spring.

North of zone 8, the winter-sweet *(Chimonanthus praecox)* requires a protected site. It will grow for several years before its small, purple-centered yellowish blooms appear. *Viburnum × bodnantense,* in contrast, reaches flowering size in a few years. It bears clusters of rose-pink flowers, scenting the air in fall and winter or very early spring.

Happy in shade, the evergreen *Mahonia bealei* bears sprays of yellow blooms scented like lily of the valley as early as January in the South, or in early spring at the northern end of zone 7.

Iris reticulata and *I. unguicularis* are delicately fragrant. The former is for the rock garden or for pots on the patio in late winter, while the latter needs poor soil and all the sun it can get.

Night scents

Several plants give off their strongest scent at dusk and later in the night. Often, they have pale tubular flowers. This group includes some lilies, honeysuckles, *Hosta plantaginea,* and the flowering tobacco — both the pale, tall forms of *Nicotiana alata* and the even taller, white-flowered *N. sylvestris.* A close relative is the angel's-trumpet *(Brugmansia suaveolens),* a tender shrub with large drooping flowers, which

▲ **Regal splendor** The glorious white trumpets of *Lilium regale* waft their spicy fragrance above a clump of aromatic artemisia 'Powys Castle,' with silvery filigree foliage. Good color contrast is provided by orache (*Atriplex hortensis* 'Rubra'), a hardy annual foliage plant.

◀ **Evening balm** Where winters are not harsh (zone 8 and south), the rich scent of white jasmine (*Jasminum officinale*) is one of the sweetest pleasures of a summer evening. A vigorous climber, the jasmine is best grown up a sturdy rustic trellis. Here, its scrambling stems, studded with clusters of white primroselike flowers, meet the silky seed heads of early-summer-flowering *Clematis macropetala*. At their feet lie neat clumps of purple-blue *Lavandula angustifolia* 'Hidcote.'

▲ **Ornamental herbs** Many aromatic herbs are decorative enough for the front of beds and borders. The scented, white-margined apple mint *(Mentha suaveolens* 'Variegata') makes a good companion for the shining leaves of golden marjoram *(Origanum vulgare* 'Aureum').

▲ **Scented ground cover**
A carpet of aromatic purple-leaved sage shows off the spires of small-flowered butterfly gladioli, whose salmon-pink blooms are splashed with orange-scarlet. Flanking the late-summer gladioli are grasslike tufts of a hybrid *Kniphofia,* topped by creamy white flower spikes.

▶ **Sweet bergamot** Also known as bee balm and Oswego tea, sweet bergamot *(Monarda didyma)* is a hardy perennial whose scarlet flowers are beloved by bees and whose aromatic leaves can be dried and used in herbal teas. Its fiery color is beautifully tempered by the silvery gray, felted foliage of lavender cotton *(Santolina chamaecyparissus).*

◀ **Miniature herb garden**
A terra-cotta pot containing golden lemon balm *(Melissa officinalis* 'Aurea') is the aromatic centerpiece in a small herb bed that includes tarragon, purple-leaved sage, and golden marjoram. Wild strawberries and sweet violets add their delicate fragrances.

▲ **Pungent sage** The strongly flavored common sage *(Salvia officinalis)* forms an attractive evergreen clump of narrow gray-green leaves. Grow several cultivars with eye-catching colored foliage together to create a delightful mounded carpet. Here, gray-green sage is fronted by purple-leaved 'Purpurascens'; white-variegated, purple-tinted 'Tricolor'; and the gold-variegated 'Icterina.'

▶ **Ground-cover herbs** In sunny situations, low-growing herbs make effective weed-smothering ground cover. Common marjoram *(Origanum vulgare)*, a perennial culinary herb, bears aromatic leaves and large clusters of rose-pink flowers throughout summer. It makes a good companion for another excellent ground-cover plant, the purple-leaved bugle *(Ajuga reptans* 'Atropurpurea').

▼ **Mediterranean mood** A soft-looking but drought-proof vista is easy to assemble with a collection of Mediterranean herbs. Here, in the background, aromatic evergreen rosemary softens the pungent odor of blue-leaved rue *(Ruta graveolens* 'Jackmans Blue') and tempers the purple-leaved *Salvia officinalis* 'Purpurascens.' Silvery lamb's tongue *(Stachys byzantina* 'Silver Carpet') and the pink flower heads of ornamental onion *(Allium karataviense)* make an attractive low edging.

▲ **Flavorful fennel** The most decorative of the culinary herbs, fennel *(Foeniculum vulgare)* is as much at home in the flower border as in the herb garden. It forms an airy bush, up to 6 ft (1.8 m) high, whose branching stems are clothed with aromatic foliage.

The bronze-leaved cultivar 'Purpureum' makes a stunning backdrop for groups of *Salvia pratensis* 'Haematodes,' whose tall stems bear lavender-blue flowers. In front, yellow-green lady's mantle *(Alchemilla mollis)* foams over the path.

scent a patio if planted in a large container. Night-scented stock *(Matthiola longipetala bicornis)* and sweet rocket *(Hesperis matronalis)* speak for themselves, as does evening primrose *(Oenothera biennis)*.

Aromatic herbs

Garden herbs are often relegated to a corner of the vegetable plot, but many bear flowers or foliage that is much too attractive to be hidden away. They are splendid when combined not only with one another but also with other partners in the ornamental garden.

Few people have room for the traditional knot garden, whose embroideries of low, interwoven hedges were often edged with sweet-scented box or artemisias and filled with aromatic and medicinal herbs. But some of these classic partnerships can be re-created in small gardens: accompanying old-fashioned shrub roses with lavender or rosemary, fragrant thyme for ground cover, and pungent sage in patio pots.

▲ **Garden hyacinths** Very hardy and available in colors ranging from white through shades of yellow, pink, red, and orange to blue and purple, fragrant garden hyacinths should be planted en masse for a showy spring display.

▼ **Scented nosegays** Dwarf cultivars of flowering tobacco *(Nicotiana alata)* are perfect for pots on the patio, where their delicious scent lingers in the summer. 'Dwarf White Bedder,' only 16 in (40 cm) high, stays open during the day.

The evergreen, blue-flowered rosemary will survive most winters in zone 7, provided it has a sunny spot, well-drained soil, and shelter from cold, drying winds. Its heady aroma fills the air on warm summer days; small sprigs are good additions to fresh and dried flower arrangements.

Chives *(Allium schoenoprasum)* make good scented edging plants for beds and borders on their own or mixed with variegated lemon-scented thyme *(Thymus × citrodorus* 'Silver Queen').

At the other end of the scale is the stately, aromatic *Angelica archangelica,* some 6 ft (1.8 m) tall. Its large leaves and domed flower heads look imposing against golden yews.

Other ornamental and fragrant herbs include the yellow-splashed ginger mint *(Mentha × gentilis* 'Variegata'), the golden lemon balm *(Melissa officinalis* 'Aurea'), and sweet bergamot *(Monarda didyma* 'Croftway Pink').

You can use aromatic herbs to scent the air indoors during winter. Many are ideal for drying and using in potpourri mixtures. Thyme, orange mint, rose geranium, lemon verbena, rosemary, and sweet marjoram hold their fragrance well.

INDEX

ACKNOWLEDGMENTS

Photo credits
Biofotos/Heather Angel 27, 51(b), 82, 97(t), 139, (Hazel le Rougetel) 71, 72(t), 74, 76(b); Michael Boys 70; Burda Magazines 151(tr); Ed Buziak 149; Brian Carter 60(br); Eric Crichton 4, 14(b), 17, 26, 30, 31(t), 40(b), 42(b), 45, 48(tr), 52(b), 53(t), 67(t), 75, 88, 89, 96, 102, 104, 106, 110, 111(b), 115(t), 118, 119, 120(t), 125, 133, 135, 136(tr), 137, 138, 141, 144, 148(tl), 160, 161, 162(t), 164(bl), 165(c), 165(b), 166(t), 169(b), 172(b); Arnaud Descat 11, 22(t), 59(br), 84, 142; Derek Fell 48, 69(t), 156; Philippe Ferret 92(t), 93(t), 107, 108(b), 112, 126, 134–135; Garden Picture Library 20(b), (Brian Carter) 34(t), 41, 91, 98(b), 152, 170, (Perdereau/Thomas) 12(t), 20(tl), 44, (David Russel) 128(t), (J. Siras) 153, (R. Sutherland) 10(t), 121(t), 150(tl), 151(br), 154, (D. Willery) 169(t), (S. Wooster) 94, 148(tr);

John Glover 18(t), 28, 29(t), 33(br), 35(t), 80, 113, 162(b), 165(t); Derek Gould 50(c); Pamela Harper 136(tl); Jerry Harpur 6, 69(b), 73(t), 109, 111(t), 129, 130, 143, 145, 157, (Magnus Ramsey) 127(b); Rob Herwig 51(t); Saxon Holt 31(b); Images Colour Library 164(br); Lamontagne 23(t), 33(t), 72(b), 92(bl), 92–93(b); Andrew Lawson 12(b), 16(tr), 36(t), 56, 59(t), 68, 98(t), 148(b); S. & O. Mathews 46(b), 65, 66(t), 114, 116, 121(b); Tania Midgley 1, 13, 14(t), 18(b), 52(t), 53(b), 66–67(b), 73(b), 79, 158–159; Natural Image (Bob Gibbons) 20(tr), 62(t), (R. Fletcher) 34–35(b); Clive Nichols front cover, 3, 46(t), 47(tr), 47(b), 78, 99, 168, back cover; Muriel Orans 21(t); Perdereau/Thomas 25, 38, 39, 42(t), 43, 47(tl), 48(tl), 60(bl), 81, 83, 85, 86, 87, 105, 108(t), 140, 172(t); Photos Horticultural 9, 19, 21(b), 22(b), 24, 29(b), 32, 33(bl), 35(b), 36(b), 49, 50(t), 50(b), 51(c), 54, 57, 59(bl), 60(t), 93(br), 95, 97(b), 100, 117, 120(b), 122, 127(t), 128(b),

131, 132, 146, 147, 150(bl), 150–151; Harry Smith Collection 10(b), 16(tl), 34(bl), 58, 62(b), 64(t), 69(t), 90, 115(b), 163(t), 166(b), 167; Jean-Paul Soulier 101; Elizabeth Whiting & Associates 40(t), (Karl-Dietrich Buhler) 8, 124.

Illustrators
Leonora Box 27, 40, 103, 104, 138(b); Wendy Bramell 64(b), 82; Lynn Chadwick 137; Colin Emberson 15(t), 28, 43; Sarah Fox-Davies 39, 163(t); Delyth Jones 10, 14, 16, 91; Nikki Kemball 11, 64(t), 79; Reader's Digest 17, 18, 19, 44, 55, 62, 66, 67, 68, 76, 80, 84, 88, 99, 106, 107, 110, 112, 134, 135, 136, 141, 144, 146, 167; Helen Senior 9, 63; Sally Smith 13, 45; Gill Tomblin 15(b), 56, 61, 94, 114, 126, 129, 132, 163(b), 164, 171; Barbara Walker 12, 25, 116, 130, 131; Ann Winterbotham 138(t).

Index compiled by Sydney Wolfe Cohen